G000055162

Releasers of Life

Discover the River Within

Releasers of Life

Discover the River Within

Mary Audrey Raycroft

© Copyright 1998 — Mary Audrey Raycroft

All rights reserved. This book is protected under the copyright laws of the United States of America. This book may not be copied or reprinted for commercial gain or profit. The use of short quotations or occasional page copying for personal or group study is permitted and encouraged. Permission will be granted upon request. Unless otherwise identified, Scripture quotations are from the HOLY BIBLE, NEW INTERNATIONAL VERSION®. NIV®. Copyright © 1973, 1978, 1984 by International Bible Society. Used by permission of Zondervan Publishing House. All rights reserved.

Scripture quotations marked AMP are taken from the Amplified Bible, Expanded Edition, copyright © 1987 by the Zondervan Corporation and the Lockman Foundation. Those marked KJV are taken from the King James Version of the Bible. Those denoted as The Message are from Eugene H. Peterson's *The Message* (Colorado Springs, CO: NavPress Publishing Group, 1993).

Emphasis within Scripture quotations is the author's own.

Take note that the name satan and related names are not capitalized. We choose not to acknowledge him, even to the point of violating grammatical rules.

Destiny Image® Publishers, Inc.
P.O. Box 310
Shippensburg, PA 17257-0310

"Speaking to the Purposes of God for This Generation
and for the Generations to Come"

ISBN 1-56043-198-9

For Worldwide Distribution
Printed in the U.S.A.

First Printing: 1998   Second Printing: 1998

This book and all other Destiny Image, Revival Press,
and Treasure House books are available
at Christian bookstores and distributors worldwide.

For a U.S. bookstore nearest you, call **1-800-722-6774**.
For more information on foreign distributors, call **717-532-3040**.
Or reach us on the Internet: **http://www.reapernet.com**

Dedication

To my husband Bill, a wonderful, patient, wise, servant-hearted man who, from the early days of our marriage, has blessed me to grow as an individual. He has encouraged me all the way, standing with me in challenging times, and lately has released me to embrace the ministry on a wider scale. He truly is a releaser of life!

Acknowledgments

To special pastors over the years who have lovingly modeled the life of the Spirit, teaching me and encouraging me to take hold of God's opportunities with faith and boldness: Bernard Warren, Ron Armstrong, Jim Doyle, Gerrit Verstraete, Brian Mahood, Gordon Grieve, and John Arnott.

To my constant, dear friend and mentor, Mary V. Goddard, who taught me about the "gifts of the Spirit" and booted me out of my comfort zone into ministry.

To the five specific "prophets" who each, unknown to the other, saw and declared the conception and birth of this book as a tool to bring liberty to God's daughters worldwide.

To my faithful friends who not only daily assist me in the work of the ministry, but who also continually support me and stand in the gap as intercessors.

To those ministers and authors who broke the ground for me and confirmed many things about women in ministry that had been in my heart for years, but which I hesitated to speak of until now:

Dr. John T. Bristow: *What Paul Really Said About Women*
Charles Trombley: *Who Said Women Can't Teach?*
Katherine Bushnell: *God's Word to Women*
L.E. Maxwell: *Women in Ministry*
Aida B. Spencer: *Beyond the Curse*
Don Rousu: Vineyard Christian Fellowship, Edmonton, AB

To Stephen Nance, who took my transcripts and blended them into a book that "sounds like me."

To the Destiny Image team who move in anointing, integrity, and vision for the Kingdom of God.

Contents

Foreword

I have known Mary Audrey Raycroft and her husband Bill for more than 25 years. She is a vivacious, generous, and full-of-life person who has always been in love with the Lord and His Church. I remember how pleased I was when in 1993 she agreed to join our pastoral staff, overseeing our Equipping Ministries and our Women's Ministry. Little did either of us know at the time how the power of the Holy Spirit, which was soon to descend upon us, would radically change our lives. She has always been a "releaser of life" ever since I've known her.

As a very gifted teacher, she has taught hundreds through her many classes on the gifts of the Spirit and Born Free sessions, and so her ministry of being a releaser of Divine life is something that is time-tested and proven over many years with many folks. She is a wonderful role model for women who are called to minister, and a great personal friend to my wife Carol and I.

Releasers of Life describes how all believers are designed to be vessels through whom God wants to pour out

His river of life into a very needy world. It defines the basis of our freedom in Christ and the key to intimacy with Him: abiding day by day. The various hindrances, pitfalls, and self-defeating mind-sets that prevent so many believers from walking in spiritual freedom and victory are spelled out, along with guidelines for avoiding them. Throughout, this book is anchored firmly in the Word of God.

The role of women in the life and ministry of the Body of Christ is a long-neglected, much misunderstood, and highly controversial area of Church life that needs to be examined closely. The Spirit of God is adjusting the Church and changing the way we look at many things. For this reason, Mary Audrey's book is important reading not just for women, but for men as well (including pastors and other ministerial staff), and for discipleship groups and youth groups.

Millions of Christian women live in bondage and defeat, ignorant of the truth of who they really are in Christ: children of a loving heavenly Father.

As senior pastor of the Toronto Airport Christian Fellowship, I have seen firsthand the lasting fruit of Mary Audrey's ministry in Toronto as she oversees areas of teaching and training. She is also an approved and effective ambassador of God's work on an international scale as she has conducted teaching and healing ministries in North America, Asia, Europe, the British Isles, the Caribbean, and Australia.

Releasers of Life is Mary Audrey's latest resource tool for awakening believers of all denominations worldwide to their freedom and calling in Christ. I highly recommend it to you.

John Arnott
Senior Pastor
Toronto Airport Christian Fellowship

Introduction

One wintry Sunday morning, December 12, 1993, my husband Bill and I settled into our seats for the morning service at our church. We were anticipating a wonderful time in the presence of God and some real challenges to the quality of our walk in Him, as the guest speaker was a humorous but hard-hitting prophet from California. After worship, he blessed several people with spontaneous, accurate words of knowledge and prophecy as he walked back and forth on the main floor. Then, as he turned to go up the steps to the podium for the morning message, he suddenly wheeled around, pointed at me, and shouted,

"This is all right! Have you written a book—have you done any writing yet? Are you just doing it? Is it already written? As I was walking from here, the Lord said, 'Ask her, "Have you written the book?"' "

"You will finish the book! You will put into print, into writing, that which God has put in your spirit, your heart. This is the decade of documentation. God wants you to document what He has taught you. It's

*essential to the Body of Christ; it's going to be helpful
to the Body of Christ. I'm not sure if it's going to be a
best-seller, but at least it's going to be something that
is helpful for the Body of Christ.*

*"You're going to see it—people are going to ask you
for it. It's going to be a pivotal turn in your life and
ministry where it's going to open up regions unknown
to you and people are going to say, 'Come here,' 'Come
here,' 'Come here,' from other parts of the world and
other countries. I especially saw a hand from Europe
saying, 'Come here.' I even saw a hand from the very
southern part, like in South Africa, and then Australia, the bottom of the earth, saying, 'Come here and
teach us' and 'Come here and minister to us.' "*

More words followed that were of a personal, family nature and I sat there somewhat stunned about what was said.
I had produced a small number of students' manuals that
had been sent abroad with the accompanying tapes, but
somehow I didn't think that's what was meant. As with
many prophetic words, these were set up on the shelf for future confirmation and open doors. I didn't know how it
would come about, since I couldn't see myself, with my
crazy schedule, putting a book together. Then too I did not
yet have a clue what the book would be about.

Over the next three years there were four more very
pointed prophetic encouragements that came from respected
women and men, unknown to each other, about some kind
of liberating book that would especially minister to women
but also be encouraging for men. Over this time I became
increasingly aware of the hurts, frustrations, and disappointments suffered by women that seemed rampant in the

Church at large. My eyes had never really been opened before to the "put-downs" and odd attitudes they received from non-flexible traditions that keep them in very restricted boxes. Everywhere I went, my words seemed to encourage listeners to see that women as well as men have the love, calling, empowering, acceptance, and anointing of the Holy Spirit to preach, teach, disciple, evangelize, and take God-appointed leadership not just in their churches alone, but in the world where they live.

Suddenly, this book took shape, brought forth from those precious times of teaching and exhorting others to move out of simply "playing church" into being "people of the River," releasing the Life of the Spirit as a natural expression of their faith. I wanted it to be non-religious and non-confusing; challenging for the average believer; pointing to an experiential relationship with God; and causing one to say, "Yes, that's for me!" I wanted it to show that, in Christ, with the indwelling Holy Spirit, there is deliverance and freedom from shame, defeat, excuses, and building the Kingdom of God with religious works of the flesh.

As you read *Releasers of Life*, I trust that you will be teachable and expectant; that you will feel ignited to search the Word for yourself. I pray that you will feel hope and joy as you find your hearts being healed. May you experience a fresh drawing to the Lord to seek intimacy with Him and, out of that, flow with guidance, confirmation, and anointing for your life calling.

Chapter 1

Releasers of Life—The Vision

Early in this century a young man in England planned to sail to New York to meet family and start a new life. Not being a man of means, he scrimped and saved every penny he could for weeks until he was able to purchase his ticket. He had just enough money left to buy some bread and cheese to eat during the trip.

Departure day arrived and the young man boarded the ship. In his cabin, he carefully portioned out his bread and cheese so they would last for the entire seven-day voyage. He was a shy man, and spent most of his time in his cabin reading, resting, and eating his cheese and bread. Occasionally he walked the decks, enjoying the good weather and the sea air, and observing the other passengers. Sometimes he peered through the windows of the dining room and watched them enjoying their banquets, their smorgasbords, and their fancy breakfasts.

The days proceeded in this manner until, on the last day, the ship entered New York harbor. All the passengers were on deck, excited and cheering as they passed the Statue of Liberty and got their first glimpse of their new home. The young man was on deck as well, and met one of the ship's pursers.

"How was your trip?" the purser asked. "I don't remember seeing you at any of the ship's functions. Was everything all right for you?"

"Oh yes," the young man replied. "I enjoyed the sunshine, the salt air, and sitting on deck. Then I would go to my cabin and eat my bread and cheese. After a week, they're a little hard and moldy, but that's all right."

Puzzled, the purser asked, "Why didn't you come into the dining room for your meals along with the other passengers?"

"Oh, I couldn't do that. I only had enough money to buy my ticket."

The purser replied in a horrified tone, "Sir, didn't you realize that the price of your ticket included **everything**?"

I first heard this story several years ago at a conference where Kenneth Copeland was teaching on our covenant relationship with God. At that time I was pondering deeply the great discrepancy between the unfruitful, defeated experience of the Church at large, and the empowering, overcoming life promised in Scripture. This story really put things into perspective for me. In fact, it made me groan, "Ouch!" Since then, as I have taught hundreds on the wonders of the born-again, Spirit-filled life of liberty in Christ, many men and women have come to me, often with tear-filled eyes, saying, "Why have we not heard this before?" They too have said "Ouch" as they identified with the young man in the story.

Millions of Christians today do not realize that when they came to Christ they received everything from Him—not just salvation, but the fullness of His life. These believers need to be released into the full liberty and usefulness in the Body of Christ that He intends for them to have. The vast majority of these Christians whose gifts are underutilized or un-tapped, and whose freedom in Christ is largely unrealized, are women.

Today a great responsibility rests on anyone who is anointed of God to be on the front line of releasing women into this fresh revival of life. There are tremendous needs in every area of the Church, but the really important thing is to move with what the Holy Spirit is saying to us right now. Speaking of liberty for women in the Church in such a re-leasing way, however, will cause tradition to gnash its teeth and howl loudly as the truth is proclaimed and imparted into the understanding of men and women.

Just as women literally are releasers of life by giving physical birth, so God has designed them to be releasers of **zoe** life, spiritual life, **His** life. Many women in the Church are unaware of this role that God has for them. His purpose is far greater than anything they have ever thought or dreamed of (see Eph. 3:20). The same Spirit who raised Christ from the dead lives in them (see Rom. 8:11). They have been re-created to do the good works that He pre-pared in advance for them to do (see Eph. 2:10). As their eyes are opened to these truths, they are released from ig-norance and fear. In turn, they are enabled to release that life to others. The time has come for women to be set free from religious yokes of bondage to traditions that have not glorified God.

This chapter and those that follow will explore the scrip-tural truths that lie behind this releasers of life concept, the basic heart of which can be stated quite simply:

**Women, as equally as men, have the anointing of God
and the capacity to release spoken and audible words
of life into every aspect of the Body of Christ, and to a
world that needs to hear of God's Kingdom and love.**

This is not another apologetic for women in ministry that
says, "Look, here we are. We're anointed too, you know.
Pay attention to us." Or, "No one appreciates us," or, "No
one gives us our place," etcetera, etcetera. That attitude is
old hat, stale, worn out, irritating, and ungodly. There's ever
so much more for us than that. The enemy has kept us in that
box for far too long. Enough is enough! It's time to come
out of it!

In April 1997 I had the tremendous privilege of participating in a round-table discussion at Destiny Image Publishers in Pennsylvania. Titled "A Woman's Round Table," the
event was attended by a number of well-known women
from a wide spectrum of Christian ministries and denominations. Two men from Destiny Image, Don Nori and Don Mi-
lam, also participated. The topic of discussion was the Body
of Christ, as the army of God, going forth in unity with the
whole body, not just half of it. There were black and white,
male and female present, and we quickly got past all the surface pleasantries and plunged deep into the heart of issues
that are vital to renewal in the Church today. Some of the in-
sights that came out of this meeting were so tremendous and
profound that they have helped me set the scene for what
follows in this book.

**#1 I believe there is a cry to awaken, equip, and release
women, within all denominations, into their calling
and full potential in and to the Body of Christ.**

Notice that this is not "women ministering to women," but women ministering "in and to the Body of Christ." We are in an unprecedented era of change right now. The cloud and the camp are moving. Are we as women willing to move with them? During the discussion in April, Don Nori of Destiny Image said, "One of our biggest needs is for people to learn that there is a new plateau for the Church, a higher level for her to move into, that's not going to pass away. It's not just a passing fancy."

One of the wonderful women attending this meeting was Dr. Fuchsia Pickett, who is now in her mid-80s. Obviously, age doesn't affect the anointing or call of God. Psalm 92:12 says, "The [uncompromisingly] righteous shall flourish like the palm tree [be long-lived, stately, upright, useful, and fruitful]; they shall grow like a cedar in Lebanon [majestic, stable, durable, and incorruptible]" (AMP). Verse 14 continues, "[Growing in grace] they shall still bring forth fruit in old age; they shall be full of sap [of spiritual vitality] and [rich in the] verdure [of trust, love, and contentment]" (AMP). How do you like that? Full of sap! Dr. Pickett is the embodiment of these verses.

She challenged us with the statement, "We're in the last of the last days. It's not yet totally fulfilled, but we're in a place of restoration. Christ came to undo the works of the devil. Part of that undoing is the restoration of equality between men and women. God is doing a new thing in the midst of the Body. He's not simply releasing what we've had in the past; He's preparing to explode ministry. There's an explosion coming."

Dr. Pickett noted that we are in the time prophesied in Joel 2:28, when God would pour out His Spirit on all people, and that the sons **and daughters** of God would prophesy. The time has come to acknowledge the prophetic voice coming through women. "The old was good," she said, "but God is doing a new thing with new wineskins. This is not a platform to promote the cause of women, but simply to give forth the Word of God. The Word of God can speak for itself."

#2 The Holy Spirit is revealing, through an increased understanding of the Word of God, His heart toward liberty for women in the Church.

We are called to release anointed truth into the lives of men and women. Paul said in Ephesians 5:26-27 that Christ washes the Church with the water of His Word to present her without stain or wrinkle, holy and blameless. As the Church is restored, her spots and wrinkles gone, she will be delivered from prejudice, tradition, denominationalism, and cultural hindrances.

Kelley Varner, in his book *The Three Prejudices*, reminds us that there are three things in particular in the Body of Christ today that hinder the Church from fulfilling her mandate: gender (the walls between men and women), race (the walls between blacks and whites and other skin colors), and nation (the walls between Jews and Gentiles).[1] In Galatians 3 Paul tells us that before faith came we were prisoners of the law, but faith released us from its supervision. In verses 28 and 29, Paul writes, "There is neither Jew nor Greek, slave nor free, male nor female, for you are all one in Christ Jesus. If you belong to Christ, then you are Abraham's seed, and heirs according to the promise." Now that faith has come, we are all sons of God through faith in Christ Jesus. As His children we are His heirs according to His promise. Not one of us is left out.

How many times have we read those verses and said, "I'm free from the law. I'm an heir of God. Great!" and then gone right back to the same old walk, still imprisoned in the same old attitudes of our hearts?

We need to understand God's Word and know His heart, but these things must be presented in a way we can grasp easily. I like the "KISS" principle: Keep It Simple, Sweetie. It has to be simple, or I'll walk around saying, "I don't understand this," and I won't be able to take hold of it. I trust that this book will release profound truth in a simple, down-to-earth way.

One of the men at the meeting shared a vision of a healed, restored, unique Body of Christ. He saw a three-legged stool that was very lopsided. The first leg was a white male, the second an Afro-American, and the third a woman. The second and third legs were not allowed to function, and the stool was trying to balance on the first leg alone. He later envisioned a glorious four-legged horse: men, women, Afro-Americans, and children, all moving in sync together, building the Kingdom of God. Although this vision portrayed Afro-Americans, it can apply to the racial differences in any nation.

#3 My heart desires to lift from women the weights of bondage, shame, and perceived inabilities, so they can function alongside men in declaring the Word of God and doing the works of the Kingdom.

We are going to see God's divine order re-established as women come alongside men. Note that it's "alongside," not "take over." There should never be a need for us as women to defend ourselves as the Lord brings us into a place of mutual respect. Millions of women struggle daily with deep hurt and pain, hungering and aching within for truth and reality, longing to be released and restored. They know instinctively that something isn't right, but can't grasp what it is that's wrong.

As women find their place of equality within the Church, tradition will resist strongly. We must emphasize in our walk and our attitudes how God through His Word shows equality, and not focus so often on how some abuse it. It's like trying to preach faith for healing—that God can heal, desires to heal, and intends to heal. Yet, half the time the only thing people can see is when it hasn't worked. They say, "Well, I know you're talking about healing, but Uncle Charlie died." God's heart is for healing. I know the sovereignty of God is a mighty part of it, but so many times people just look at the negative. The same is true with women not being the liberated, released, godly creatures that the Lord longs for them to be.

I do a lot of teaching on exposing "Jezebel" in the Church, which is the spirit of domination, manipulation, and control. It does need to be taught, but we spend so much of our time looking at that only. What about the Deborahs, the Huldahs, the Miriams, the Marys, the Annas, the Priscillas, and the Phoebes?

Consider Catherine Booth, Maria Woodworth-Etter, Aimee Semple-McPherson, Corrie Ten Boom, Amy Carmichael, Katherine Bushnell, Kathryn Kuhlman, Gladys Aylward, and Mother Theresa. All of these women, and many more like them, were used mightily by God in fulfilling His purpose. Why don't we lift them up as positive examples and role models?

#4 It is time to recognize that God anoints and appoints His daughters to prophesy, preach, teach, and assume leadership roles alongside His sons in the local church,

in the Body of Christ at large, and in the world, expressing humility and character, and trusting God for His promotion.

This is a truth that the Church has been slow to acknowledge. In fact, the Church has firmly resisted it for centuries. With the current river of renewal, however, the Holy Spirit is beginning to turn the tide. It is a matter of waiting for His timing. Many of us have a hard time trusting God, don't we? He has a purpose and a plan for us. Don't you think He is able to bring it about? Yet we keep saying, "Somebody isn't opening a door for me." Did you ever stop to think that maybe Somebody has not opened the door for you? Revelation 3:8 says, "I have placed before you an open door that no one can shut." This has nothing to do with trying to find places for ourselves and occupying them. God is the One who sits over the Church. He is the One who opens the doors. When God opens a door, no one except Him can shut it.

Lynn Lucas, a participant at the Destiny Image "Women's Round Table," recalled a prophetic word from the Lord, which we believe He is still saying to many women today: "You're missing the point. I'm not telling you to raise up women, but to unite men and women together to bring healing. You're called to be instruments of restoration, an army functioning together." She reminded us that although women will look, sound, and think differently than men, they are still in the same army.

God wants to instill a passion that's been missing. Ladies, for too long we have been apologetic for who we are, rather than passionate for who we are. It's time that we became passionate and thrilled about what God has done within us and how He sees us. We get so blinded by the walls of our own little boxes when He has so much more for us. The Body of Christ can't be whole with just half of it functioning.

Many of you no doubt have heard of the Azusa Street revival in Los Angeles at the beginning of the twentieth century. That profound movement of God wasn't hindered by rampant racism, ignorance, terrorism, white supremacy, opposition to education for minorities, or any of the other awful things that were going on at that time. None of that prevented the Holy Spirit from moving. At Azusa Street, gender, race, color, and nationality did not matter. The Chinese came, the Ethiopians came, and the Indians came. Mexicans and Americans came. Blacks, whites, men, women, and children—all gathered freely where the river was flowing, and worked together in unity. The color line, the class line, and the gender line were all washed away by the blood of the Lamb. Women had full rights of participation. There was equality in the Body of Christ. I long to see this in our time right now, where the anointing on each individual is looked for and respected.

The Azusa Street revival ended when the whites pulled out and started their own work. Separation began again between the races and between denominations. Liberty for women was stifled, and the divisive spirit was not dealt with.

We need to recognize this spirit of division within the Body. God brought the torch of revival to the Church at Azusa Street. It was the torch of unity, equality, and harmony in the Spirit of God. God gave it to the Church and the Church dropped it. The world picked it up, ran with it, and distorted it. If you do a bit of history you will discover that it was at this same time that many of the radical extremist movements in the world began. The Church dropped the torch and the world picked it up, giving birth to many of today's ungodly movements.

Dotty Schmitt, a pastor and tremendous revival historian, spoke of these facts at the Round Table meeting. She said that there is an unfulfilled mandate for the twentieth century that was birthed in revival at the beginning of it, and that the Lord is giving us another opportunity at the close of it.

One man I know was brought face to face with his prejudices over the issue of women's roles in ministry. He comes from a strong discipleship movement background where women were relegated to the kitchen and the bedroom with absolutely no opportunity for expression within the church, and little in the home. He thought he had dealt with his prejudices in this matter until he had some strong negative reactions to the concept that God has greater purposes for His daughters. Moving into deep repentance, he now says that this is an understanding that needs to be released to many leaders, both male and female. It is not a gender or race issue; it's about the Word of the Lord.

This likely will cause great conflict because every time God restores a truth in the Body, the old thought and the new thought collide, creating misunderstanding and division. We need to pray that this will not be a source of division, and that the Lord will raise up men who will stand and say, "We need to hear the Word of the Lord from our sisters." We need men who will stand with women, enabling them to be what God has designed and called them to be.

We need to submit to the gifting, whether it comes from a woman or a man; from a black or a white, or a cream or a yellow. The gifting, the anointing, is not dependent upon gender or race.

Marcia Ford, an associate editor for *Charisma* magazine, addressed this issue in the March 1997 magazine. In her editorial "Leaving Sexism Behind," she told the following story:

"Not long ago a pastor from a traditionally male-governed church enrolled in a course on leadership principles at a Bible college in the Atlanta area. The pastor had never heard of the instructor listed on the registration form as 'C. Driver,' but he had heard good things about the quality of the school.

"When he arrived for the first class, he found a woman standing at the podium. She was the instructor, **Carolyn** Driver.

"**Learn leadership principles from a woman? No way**, the pastor thought. All his life he had believed women were unqualified to provide spiritual direction to men. Not wanting to appear rude, the pastor decided he would stay for the first class, but would later drop the course and demand a refund.

"By the end of the first session, however, the pastor was hooked. He even forgot that he was actually listening to a **woman**. When the semester was over, the pastor organized a leadership seminar in his own church—and he asked 'C. Driver' to be the instructor.

"What did Carolyn Driver do to win this man over to a new attitude toward women in ministry? She simply did what God had called her to do, when and where He called her to do it. She also modeled female leadership in the best possible way by knowing her subject thoroughly, communicating it well, and leaving the gender issue outside the door."[2]

This same issue of *Charisma* contains articles about other women who, in Marcia Ford's words:

"...have managed to go about their Father's business without making a big fuss over gender; they aren't radical feminists with axes to grind. They're simply women who ignore the man-made road blocks designed to prevent them from carrying out the Father's will.

"Still, the road blocks exist.

"Denominations refuse to ordain women, male pastors refuse to share the pulpit with female ministers, leaders teach that Scripture prohibits women from preaching. Male leaders also insult their female counterparts with not-so-funny sexist jokes, demean women with stereotyped comments and express a bewildering amazement when they discover that some women aren't so shallow after all.

"While the church is sidetracked by all of this, people are going straight to hell."[3]

One article tells of thousands of revelers who make an annual pilgrimage to a barren desert in Northwestern Nevada to celebrate pagan rituals. Ford writes:

"Do you think it matters to Jesus who preaches the gospel to these people? If [a woman minister] had set up shop in the desert to reach the satan worshipers, would the Lord tell her she was unsuitable to rescue them from hell because of her gender? I don't think so.

"Theologians will continue to spend their time and energy debating the gender issue. But women of God who refuse to be distracted from doing the will of the Father will continue to preach, teach, minister, and serve in whatever function He requires."[4]

She concludes, "If you ever see a feature article by 'M. Ford' in *New Man* magazine, don't assume the writer is a guy named **Mark**."[5]

#5 I encourage women to be reconcilers, peacemakers, and hope-givers to tired congregations and leaders; ones who will release words of life and be nurturers, expressing that side of the nature of God that only a woman can really do well.

Not to Us

Father, You have given precious gifts from Heaven,
Equipping us to serve You as You move upon the
    earth.
You've prepared us for this hour and anointed us
    with power
For humble acts of righteousness;
We freely volunteer to do Your work.

Ambassadors of reconciliation,
Preaching the good news of Jesus Christ;
Praying for the increase of Your Kingdom;
Piercing the darkness with Your light.

Not to us, but to You be all the praises;
Not to us, but to the glory of Your grace.
We will lift up Your standard to this world
Not for us, but for the honor of Your name, O Father,
Not for us, but for the honor of Your name.

Father, You have chosen the weak and the broken;
These ones are the vessels through whom You
   command Your strength
We offer up our lives as living sacrifices
Fill us with Your Spirit now and send us out to
   bring the harvest in.
For the honor of Your name…
Restore the honor of Your name.[6]

God has given each of us precious gifts from Heaven, equipping us to serve Him as He moves upon the earth. He has given to His Church the apostle, the prophet, the evangelist, the pastor, and the teacher to equip the saints, both male and female, to do the work of the ministry (see Eph. 4:11-12 KJV). This is more than simply being in church, or making a church bigger and bigger; it is being equipped for ministry. You may be a nurse, a schoolteacher, a mom, a factory worker, a worker in a doughnut shop, or whatever. Where you are is where the work of the ministry takes place.

God has also given each of us supernatural abilities and tools to do the work of His Kingdom, as well as specific motivational gifts that make us the way we are, unique and different from everyone else. He has prepared us for this hour. Now is the time. Now is the day of salvation. Now is the day of renewal. Now is the day when the river is flowing. We have an abiding relationship with Him right now.

The current renewal is opening doors that we've never seen before. God has anointed us with His power for humble acts of righteousness for doing the works of the Kingdom. In John 14:12 Jesus says, "I tell you the truth, anyone who has faith in Me will do what I have been doing. He will do even greater things than these, because I am going to the Father." And in Acts 1:8 He says, "But you will receive power when the Holy Spirit comes on you; and you will be My witnesses in Jerusalem, and in all Judea and Samaria, and to the ends of the earth.''

"You will **be** My witnesses.'' That's a big word, **be**. Our very lives will be a witness to the fact that the Lord Jesus Christ is resurrected from the dead. The same Spirit who raised Him from the dead lives in us, and it is He who will pour out of us as a River of Life, everywhere we are. It cannot be stifled by another human being. Only our own disobedience can cut off the flow.

We must freely volunteer to do His work. He's releasing such servant's hearts within us. We should be like David when he said, "...Your law is my delight" (Ps. 119:77). We should delight to do His will. The apostle Paul tells us in Second Corinthians 5:19-20 that we are Christ's ambassadors of reconciliation. Reconciliation means the restoration of a proper, loving, interpersonal relationship that has been broken or disrupted. An ambassador represents a ruling authority and is chosen from the ranks of the mature and experienced. We must be spiritually mature to be effective ambassadors for Christ. All of us are at different levels of maturity. Whatever level we are at, we need to be ambassadors for Him, reconciling others to Jesus Christ, speaking of His love, liberty, and life.

Jesus stood in the synagogue one day and said, "The Spirit of the Lord is on Me..." (Lk. 4:18). Well, the Spirit of the Lord is on us too, women as well as men. He's been poured out upon us for preaching the gospel to the poor (both the physically and spiritually poor) and proclaiming liberty to the captives in every area of life, as well as recovery of sight to the blind in every area of blindness. He is our lover. He is our liberator. In Christ Jesus there is neither slave nor free, Jew nor Greek, male nor female (see Gal. 3:28). We are all one in Him. That's good news.

Being a reconciler also means praying for the increase of God's Kingdom. Romans 14:17 says, "For the kingdom of God is not a matter of eating and drinking, but of righteousness, peace and joy in the Holy Spirit." Paul tells the Corinthians, "For the kingdom of God is not a matter of talk but of power" (1 Cor. 4:20). If it were just a matter of talk, North America should be the most spiritual continent on the face of the earth because we've had lots of it. Pray for the increase of His Kingdom in size, as souls are won to Christ. Pray also for an increased awareness within ourselves of righteousness and holiness so that our lives will count for Him, and that the Kingdom of God will be seen in the Church and manifested in the world.

The Holy Spirit is going to pierce our darkness with His light. Light dispels darkness and brings understanding. It exposes fear and ignorance. Many of these will be pierced by the sword of the Lord, the Word of God. We will grasp His truths in our hearts and, seeing the truth of His divine order, will break free from ignorance, fear, and apology. His light will pierce the places of our self-protection and self-promotion, and He alone will get the credit for anything accomplished. We will lift up His standard. The world will finally see the Church of Jesus Christ as the wonder He designed it to be, a community of love and grace and full of life and power, not a boring, ineffective club that draws no interest and offers no hope.

God chooses the weak and the broken as His vessels through which He commands strength. In the wonderful, fragile clay pots of our lives He manifests His life. Paul tells us in Romans 12:1 to offer our bodies to God as living sacrifices.

We offer up our bodies, our faculties, our emotions, and everything that we know about ourselves in a day-by-day submission to Him. He fills us with His Spirit and sends us out to bring the harvest in.

What standard is being raised before our families and communities, our cities and our nations? What kingdom or platform is being promoted? We need to search our hearts and ask the Holy Spirit to reveal any selfish or worldly agendas. Then we need to say, "Lord, I reckon myself dead to that and alive to You," so that it can be torn down. May we never give the enemies of God opportunity to despise and blaspheme Him. Proclaim His awesomeness through living the liberty He releases us into. Paul calls this our spiritual act of worship as we stop being conformed to the same old ways, and are transformed by having our minds renewed by the Lord.

What a vision we are receiving—to be awesome, God-filled releasers of life!

Endnotes

1. Kelley Varner, *The Three Prejudices* (Shippensburg, PA: Destiny Image Publishers, 1997), Preface.

2. Marcia Ford, "Leaving Sexism Behind," *Charisma* (March 1997), 6.

3. Ford, "Leaving Sexism Behind."

4. Ford, "Leaving Sexism Behind."

5. Ford, "Leaving Sexism Behind."

6. Robert Critchley, "Not to Us" © 1996, Wild Ox Publishing. Used by permission.

Chapter 2

The River Within

I've got a river of life flowing out of me
Makes the lame to walk and the blind to see
Opens prison doors, sets the captive free
I've got a river of life flowing out of me.
Spring up, O well within my soul
Spring up, O well and make me whole
Spring up, O well and give to me
That life abundantly.

That little chorus has been around for a long time, but it speaks to a truth that we really need to tap into if we are going to be releasers of life.

Over the past several years, during this time of renewal and revival, there has been a lot of talk about the river—the river of God, standing in the river, flowing in the river, letting the river pour over us. It's like we are expecting some great awesome tidal wave to come. I don't have a clue what this next move is going to be like, but I think I've been looking for something to come from "without."

Lately, though, God has caused me to do a lot of thinking about this river. We keep hearing about the river of God pouring out upon the face of the earth, but it seems that there is only a trickle. Let's think about this. If the Holy Spirit who anoints both the corporate Body of Christ and individuals is also the One who abides and remains within us, then what would happen if we as believers began to allow His life to pour out of us like a river individually and corporately? Can you imagine what it would look like? Can you just imagine what the Church would look like if we were all flowing as a river? Maybe you have never thought about it that way, but I am more and more convinced that the river is not going to come from without, but from *within*.

If we are to be releasers of life, we must discover the river within. That river is Jesus—His life in us, pouring out of us from the very depths of our being.

Jesus Is the River

It was the last and greatest day of the Feast of the Tabernacles. Jesus stood in the Temple court and shouted:

> ... *"If anyone is thirsty, let him come to Me and drink. Whoever believes in Me, as the Scripture has said, streams of living water will flow from within him"* (John 7:37-38).

Why did Jesus say this? What did He mean?

The Feast of the Tabernacles was a joyous, week-long festival that followed the Day of Atonement, a sober time of confession and repentance. It celebrated the presence of God in the midst of His people, as represented first by the tabernacle that the Israelites had set up in the desert. For seven days, Jewish families lived in small booths constructed of twigs of myrtle, willow, and palm woven together. These temporary structures were reminders of the booths the Israelites had lived in after the Exodus and symbolized not privation and misery, but protection and preservation.

Each morning during the festival, a wild, joyful procession of dancing, jumping, shouting, laughing, rejoicing, and waving of palm and willow branches followed the priests as they filled a golden pitcher with water from the pool of Siloam in Jerusalem and carried it to the altar. There, at the time of the morning sacrifice, the water was poured out on the altar as an offering to God while the people continued to shout and sing. It symbolized the water that poured from the rock that Moses struck in the desert to satisfy the thirst of the Israelites. During the procession, as they had for hundreds of years, the people recited from the scroll of Isaiah:

> *"Surely God is my salvation; I will trust and not be afraid. The Lord, the Lord, is my strength and my song; He has become my salvation." With joy you will draw water from the wells of salvation* (Isaiah 12:2-3).

Consider the scene. John records that Jesus came to the celebration in secret. Many people were looking for Him for the wrong reasons, including some who wanted to kill Him. Halfway through the festival He appeared at the Temple court and began to teach. On the final day, amid the noisy, joyful procession, and as the water from the pool of Siloam was poured out on the altar, Jesus stood and made His surprising statement. He "said in a loud voice." He shouted. In other words, He got everyone's attention. Then He compared Himself to that rock in the desert, and to the water that flowed from it. He was its source. Anyone who believed in Him would find rivers of living water flowing from within. John 7:38 in the Amplified Bible says:

He who believes in Me [who cleaves to and trusts in and relies on Me] as the Scripture has said, From his innermost being shall flow [continuously] springs and rivers of living water (John 7:38 AMP).

The apostle Paul identified Christ as the rock that was broken open, from which the water flowed. Referring to the Israelites in the desert, he wrote:

They all ate the same spiritual food and drank the same spiritual drink; for they drank from the spiritual rock that accompanied them, and that rock was Christ (1 Corinthians 10:3-4).

When Jesus calls to anyone who is thirsty, He calls to anyone who has an ardent, eager, famishing, all-consuming craving and passion of the soul for complete union with God in the fullness of the Spirit. That sounds thirsty. When He says, "Come to Me and drink," He means complete surrender to the will of God and wholehearted reception of the gifts, fruit, and operations of the Holy Spirit.

People of the River

How thirsty are we? Are we thirsty just for a good renewal meeting, or for the very presence of the Lord Jesus Christ? Are we thirsty only for a good feeling, and manifestations of the Spirit, or for the full river within? I think God is bringing us to the place where we have to ask ourselves how thirsty we really are.

There is a river within each of us who have received the in-filling of the Holy Spirit. Is it pouring out? Is the river pouring out as God intends it to, or is it no more than a trickle, or even dammed up completely? Is the in-filling of the Holy Spirit a one-time event in our lives for our convenience and occasional use for help with ministry, or is there more to it than that?

I believe that the Lord wants His Church to be people of the river. **Christians should be river people. Releasers of life should be river people.** What does it mean to be a man or woman of the river? Is it different from what we have seen coming from the Church before?

I have spoken many times about the river pictured in Ezekiel 47:1-12. The prophet describes a river that gets progressively deeper—ankle-deep, knee-deep, waist-deep, and finally, too deep to stand up in. This represents increasing levels of immersion in the life and presence of God. Knee-deep is the place of prayer, a place of submission to the Lord. Waist-deep is where fruitfulness begins. The full depth of the river means total trust and dependence on God. Life thrives in abundance on the banks of the river: "swarms of living creatures," "large numbers of fish," "fruit trees of all kinds," with leaves that do not wither and which bear fruit every month, all because the river flows constantly from God's sanctuary. Indeed, "where the river flows everything will live" (Ezek. 47:9,12).

What would happen if we in the Church truly caught the vision of the river within—if we believed it 100 percent, then walked in it, expected it, and manifested it? Manifestations of the Lord's presence touching our frail bodies are wonderful and awesome, but how about a manifestation of God's river pouring out of us that makes the world sit up and take notice? Perhaps God has broken in upon our lives, our churches, our traditions, and our structures in such a phenomenal way so that **we** will sit up and take notice, and truly become river people through whom His life pours. He's tired of us playing church.

Made for a Purpose

If we are to be people of the river, then we need to walk as new creatures in Christ who have been made for a purpose. We have been created as vessels to contain Him. We are containers designed to hold and pour out the very life of God. As Christians, we experienced a life-changing miracle. God chose us before time began and called us according to His purpose. Now He wants to mold us into the image of Jesus, who is that river, and who desires to pour out of us.

Paul referred to this river of the presence of Christ when he wrote to the Corinthians, "But we have this treasure in jars of clay to show that this all-surpassing power is from God and not from us" (2 Cor. 4:7). In the culture of Paul's day, it was common for people to hide their most valuable possessions, their money or jewels or such, in common clay pots. This was their security system. The "treasure" of the presence and power of Christ is held in the "jars of clay," frail human bodies, so that when it pours out, there is no doubt that it comes from God and not man.

In Christ, then, we are just a bunch of wonderful pots designed to house His glory. That doesn't mean imitating Him. None of us could imitate Jesus no matter how hard we tried. That would just be the flesh trying to do godly works. No, it means being changed; it means learning to become a free, open, and totally surrendered vessel for Him to pour His life through. If we would only begin to see ourselves that way, what a difference it would make. All the sweat and the striving and the pressure to produce would just drop away. The Holy Spirit wants to manifest His life through you and me. Our part is to make ourselves available for Him to use, to be a willing body.

We are "jars of clay" designed as dwelling places for the Holy Spirit. When each of us came to Christ, the Holy Spirit took up permanent residence inside us. He is there to pour out the gifts, the ministry, the power, the love, and the word of God through us. This is a continual fulfillment of Jesus' promise in John 14:16-17 that the Father would send "another Counselor...the Spirit of truth," to live with us forever.

When Jesus spoke those words to His disciples, He was preparing them for a new dimension of experience. For three years they had followed Him, watching, learning, and enjoying His constant physical presence. All of this had been external, however. Now He was going away and would not be with them any longer. What would they do without Him? Jesus promised that He would not leave them as orphans. He would come to them, but not in the same way as before. The disciples had been with Jesus, and the Spirit of God had been with them, but from now on the Spirit would be **in** them (see Jn. 14:17). They would experience the presence of God in a totally new and different way.

After the resurrection Jesus fulfilled His promise. John 20:19-22 records that Jesus appeared to His disciples, breathed on them, and said, "Receive the Holy Spirit." I believe that action was similar to what God did to Adam originally when He breathed into him the breath of life. The inference here is that Jesus went from disciple to disciple, almost like mouth to mouth resuscitation, and imparted the Holy Spirit to them.

The Holy Spirit is the very resurrection life of Jesus. Paul wrote in Romans 8:11 that "...the Spirit of Him who raised Jesus from the dead is living in you...." Think about that! The same Spirit, the same power that raised Jesus from the dead, lives in us!

Surely this must mean something. Once, after I had been teaching on the Spirit and the gifts, a woman came up to me and said, "If it's true that the same Spirit that raised Christ from the dead lives in us, how come we're such a bunch of limp noodles?"

It is because of ignorance. We don't know who we really are in the Lord. We don't understand what His Word says about us. There are thousands and thousands of Christians who haven't got a clue about what happened when they were born again. They embraced the Christian faith, and they believe that if they hang on tightly and live a good life until Jesus comes back, then their "fire insurance" is all paid up and they're fine. What more do they need?

We are so ignorant about the purposes and the heart of God—about what He's building and about His Body and His Bride. We have been made for a purpose. God loves us passionately, but in that love lies a purpose for us to move in, and it has nothing to do with works. His purpose is for us to be releasers of His life—the mighty, abundant, ever-flowing river of His resurrection life.

There are two kinds of life: **bios** and **zoe**. *Bios* is the natural, physical life we share with all other creatures. *Zoe* is spiritual life, God's life. So many times we try to do the works of the Kingdom, live as Christians, and express the life of the Spirit, but we try to do so in the strength of *bios*, our natural life. That is why we are so often weak, defeated, and ineffective. Oswald Chambers, in his classic devotional book, *My Utmost for His Highest*, expresses this beautifully:

"The expression of Christian character is not good doing, but God-likeness. If the Spirit of God has transformed you within, you will exhibit Divine characteristics in your life, not good human characteristics. God's life in us expresses itself as **God's** life, not as human life trying to be godly. The secret of a Christian is that the supernatural is made natural in him by the grace of God, and the experience of this works out in the practical details of life, not in times of communion with Him."[1]

God's life in us will express itself as God's life. We don't have to turn Him on one little bit. He's always "on." We're the ones who need to be turned on! We are simply vessels through whom He wants to pour His river of life. We were made for that purpose.

Chosen by God

I was surprised when I finally read John 15:16 with some understanding, where Jesus said:

You did not choose Me, but I chose you and appointed you to go and bear fruit—fruit that will last. Then the Father will give you whatever you ask in My name (John 15:16).

I had always thought that I chose Him. He says we didn't choose Him, but He chose us. He appointed us, planted us, and poured His Spirit into us that we might bear lasting fruit. When we are fruitful, the Father is honored and glorified, and we prove ourselves to be true followers of Christ. He did not come just to improve our behavior. The truth is that we are completely new individuals. We are children of God. Christ Himself is our life. The very seed, the very life of God, His very own nature, is within us.

I think Romans 5:5 illustrates this quite well: "...God has poured out His love into our hearts by the Holy Spirit, whom He has given us." Picture Niagara Falls, where millions of gallons of water rush by every second. Such a huge deluge of water is called a cataract. That is what Paul is saying in this verse: "God has 'cataracted' His love into our hearts." We are partakers of His divine nature.

The Holy Spirit is the one who brings into action the life and the fruit that we have been created to bear. We are fruit-bearers, not fruit-producers. We bear the fruit that the Holy Spirit produces in us. We are vessels made to carry His life. That is the fruit of righteousness, the fruit of being in right standing with Him.

Not very long ago, another leader challenged me in this area. We were talking about ways in which the Christian life was being manifested, and how people's lives would change. Being an exhorter, I kept saying, "We should be out there. We should be exercising the gifts of the Spirit. We should be healing the sick. We should be praying for people." We should this and we should that. He said that it is not a matter of "should." Anything we do because we "should" is an act of the flesh. The fruit and the river must flow as natural outpourings of the supernatural life within us. It's not something we have to "get out and do." If we could learn to rest in the Lord and simply bear the fruit that He produces in us, what a difference it would make. It would certainly remove a lot of pressure.

The Word says that we were planned for and chosen by God from before the beginning of time, called according to His purpose and design, to be molded into the very image of the Lord Jesus Christ (see Eph. 1:4; Rom. 8:28-29). That's you and me, with all our hang-ups and our bad hair days. In everything, God is working in our lives to conform us more and more into the likeness of Christ. Sometimes we beg or plead or scream for God to do something about our circumstances. He may change them, or He may choose to change us in the midst of them. Whatever comes into our lives, good or bad, God will take it, turn it, and use it to change us more and more into His likeness.

A friend of mine recently found an original Webster's dictionary published in the nineteenth century. Noah Webster, a Christian, defined **religion** as "a return to bondage." You and I don't have a religion. I hate that word with a passion. We don't have religion—we have Life. Religion is man's attempt to reach out and find God and earn His favor. Christianity is God reaching down to us, pouring out His life for us to restore us to His own heart. Religion is form and ritual, legalism and tradition. Christianity is life and relationship with the living God. Religion is centered on man's efforts. Christianity is based on God's initiative. There's all the difference in the world between the two.

As Christians, we are not simply men and women who embrace the Christian religion. We are God's chosen children, and I long to see us truly walk in that reality.

New Creations

Some of you may say, "That's all fine and good. I'm chosen by God, but how can I live this kind of spiritual life, this **zoe** life of God? After all, what do you expect? I'm only human."

No, you're not. As a Christian, by virtue of being born again, the Spirit of Christ lives within you and you are a totally new creature. The apostle Paul stated it this way:

"Therefore, if anyone is in Christ, he is a new creation; the old has gone, the new has come!" (2 Cor. 5:17) Once you were in Adam, the old man; now you are in Christ. The Spirit of the living God dwells within you, along with all the resources of Heaven. So, you are more than "only human."

The Word tells us that we are God's own workmanship. Ephesians 2:10 in the Amplified Bible says:

For we are God's [own] handiwork (His workman-ship), recreated in Christ Jesus, [born anew] that we may do those good works which God predestined (planned beforehand) for us [taking paths which He prepared ahead of time], that we should walk in them [living the good life which He prearranged and made ready for us to live].

Nothing surprises God. He knows exactly where we are, what we are doing, what our circumstances are, and what lies ahead for us. He puts us in situations that stretch us, challenging us to stand in our faith and trust Him as He brings us into a new way of walking.

Hebrews 6:9 talks about the good fruit that accompanies salvation. John 15:16 says that Christ chose us that we might bear lasting fruit. Earlier in the same chapter Jesus gives the parable of the vine and the branches. He is the Vine, the source of life and fruit. We are the branches who partake of the life of the Vine, and bear His fruit. This is pos-sible only as we abide in the Vine. This abiding, discussed in greater detail in Chapter 5, is an act of the Spirit, not of the flesh. It is not something we do in our own strength, but is a position of resting in His grace.

Chosen by God, bearing the fruit of the Spirit, abiding in Christ; all of these mark our identity as new creatures in the

Lord. God did not save us simply to improve our behavior. Let me remind you again, we are not talking about behavior modification here, but a complete transformation. In Christ we have been totally remade, brand-new from the inside out.

God has made us new creations so that we may do the works of Christ. First Peter 2:9 says:

But you are a chosen race, a royal priesthood, a dedicated nation, [God's] own purchased, special people, that you may set forth the wonderful deeds and display the virtues and perfections of Him Who called you out of darkness into His marvelous light (AMP).

In John 14:12 Jesus told His disciples:

I tell you the truth, anyone who has faith in Me will do what I have been doing. He will do even greater things than these, because I am going to the Father.

What are the works of Christ? We get all excited about the "greater things than these" when we need to get busy simply doing what He did—opening blind eyes and deaf ears, casting out demons, raising the dead, and preaching the good news of the Kingdom of God. Once we start doing the same things, then we can feel comfortable moving on to the greater things. It doesn't matter how old we are, what our backgrounds are, or whether we are male or female. He made us for this, that He might pour out the river of His life through us.

If the Church began to manifest the supernatural life of the risen Lord, we would not be able to keep people from our doors. They would know where to come to get their hearts healed, their bodies healed, their demons delivered, and their dead spirits, souls, and bodies raised.

Equipped for Ministry

The ministry of the Church is described in Ephesians 4:11-13:

It was He who gave some to be apostles, some to be prophets, some to be evangelists, and some to be pastors and teachers, **to prepare God's people for works of service**, *so that the body of Christ may be built up until we all reach unity in the faith and in the knowledge of the Son of God and become mature, attaining to the whole measure of the fullness of Christ.*

All of us as Christians are called to the works of the ministry. None of us are excluded. God has chosen us, anointed us, empowered us, and equipped us for "works of service" to build up the Body of Christ and proclaim Him to the lost. Our empowering comes from the Holy Spirit. As we grow in our knowledge of who we are in Christ and of the purpose for which He made us, and learn to open ourselves up to Him, His river of power and blessing and life will pour out of us like a flood.

What does the Holy Spirit do in our lives? He comforts us, dwells within us, teaches us, and brings the things of God to our remembrance. He convicts us, guides us, and reveals God's will to us. He worships with us and works to produce the character of Christ in us. He gives us the victory that Jesus won for us. He compensates for our weaknesses. He strengthens us, assists us, exhorts us, encourages us, counsels us, and advises us. He steps into difficult situations and defends us. He brings joy. He brings gifts and fruit, and righteousness, peace, and power. He gives us boldness and hope. He gives us the words to speak and helps us preach the gospel.

Can you see how truly great a "treasure" we have in our "jars of clay"? God has equipped us for everything He wants us to do. There is nothing that we cannot accomplish. He has placed all the resources of Heaven at our disposal. It is not for us, however, to try to do these things in our own strength or for our own benefit. It is only through His power, by walking in His Spirit, that we can live and minister in a way that makes a difference. Remember Philippians 2:13, "For it is God who works in you to will and to act according to His good purpose," and Philippians 4:13, "I can do everything through Him who gives me strength."

God doesn't call the qualified; He qualifies the called. So feeling inadequate or unworthy is not really the issue because He has called you and qualified you, and He wants to bring you to the point of being totally confident in His ability to enable you to be a releaser of life. You are born again. Hopefully you are Spirit-baptized and empowered for service. The Holy Spirit has taken up residence within you, and His life, abilities, and anointing are available to you.

Jesus said, "As the Father has sent Me, I am sending you" (Jn. 20:21b). Consider then that you have been made, designed, called, and chosen for the very purpose of displaying the river of God in your life. Blessing and helping people, healing their diseases, building them up in the Word, breaking the power of the adversary over their lives, teaching them how to live in the Father's will and to walk daily in a fearless and glorious fellowship with Him; these are the good works planned by the Father for us to walk in.

The Book of Acts is not finished. We are still living in the Acts of the Apostles. We are still living in the Acts of the Holy Spirit. He did not stop manifesting Himself and pouring

Himself out when the last apostle died. He is still here for us and in us. We need to become Acts 29 people, pouring out the river of God to our world. He made us for that purpose.

Endnote

1. Oswald Chambers, *My Utmost for His Highest* (New York: Dodd, Mead and Company, 1935), 264.

Chapter 3

The Basis of Our Freedom

We have been made for a purpose, chosen by God, and equipped for ministry in order that He might pour out His life through us to the world. If this is God's design and plan for us, why do so many of us experience a different reality? Why is the Christian experience for so many one of fear, fruitlessness, bondage, and defeat? I believe that it is because many Christians do not understand one of the most basic realities of life in Christ: freedom. Jesus Christ has set us free. What does that mean? Understanding our freedom in Christ will open up for us a whole new world of almost infinite possibilities.

The basic Scripture regarding our freedom in Christ is Romans 8:1-2:

Therefore, there is now no condemnation for those who are in Christ Jesus, because through Christ Jesus the law of the Spirit of life set me free from the law of sin and death.

Notice what Paul is saying here. First of all, if we are in Christ, there is no condemnation. That means no guilt, no judgment, and no eternal consequences for our sin. All of that has been washed away by His blood. Through Christ a new law is operating in our lives: the law of life in the Spirit. That law has liberated us from the old law of sin and death with its legalism, rules, and bondage to tradition and dead-end religion. Christ has set us free to become everything He wants us to be, and He has the power and desire to bring it about.

We have been born of God to be free. Freedom is something we all desire—freedom to be our real selves, and to enjoy life, God, and others; freedom to receive and give love, forgiveness, and acceptance; freedom to "pull out all the stops" of life and minister with boldness, courage, and fruitfulness. Is such freedom possible for us? Does the Lord really have this kind of life in mind for us?

Free in Christ?

Years ago, Lloyd John Ogilvie, a Presbyterian pastor, taught that we have the right to be free in and through Jesus. He called it our "rebirth right." Christ has given us our rebirth right, and we need the confidence to step forward and boldly claim it. If it is true that we are free in Christ from the law of sin and death, then we have an obvious problem. The sad reality is that so many Christians do not live in that freedom on a day-to-day basis. For many of us, what was promised has not come to pass in practical reality in our lives. Maybe it is that way with you. Pastor Ogilvie continued to state that it is a fact that many of us who claim the name of Christ feel and act no more free than those who make no pretense of faith. We have the same hang-ups, the same frustrations and anxieties, and the same self-consciousness:

What will people think of me? We are tied down by the same feelings of guilt. We get uptight over winning other people's approval. We are wiped out by criticism and negative opinions. We are restricted by our own self-doubt, caution, and fear and subject ourselves to mental torment of every kind. In practical reality then, what is the difference between us and someone who doesn't even name the name of Jesus?

Pastor Ogilvie brought forth some thought-provoking questions and truths. What things in your life prevent you from feeling and acting free in Christ? Perhaps it is fear of failure or fear of rejection. It may be self-consciousness or insecurity. Maybe it is lack of faith or boldness, or ignorance of God's Word. Perhaps there is a deep sense of guilt or anxiety or worry. There may be past abuses that you cannot put behind you. You may be harboring unforgiveness over a past hurt. Any of these conditions, and countless others like them, will hinder your ability to exercise the freedom Christ died to give you. Whatever they are, they reflect thoughts and attitudes of a sinful world, and stand contrary to the Word of God.

The truth is, we act according to the way we think. On the other hand, true spiritual freedom is rooted in God's unchangeable, incorruptible Word. All the thoughts and emotions that make us feel unfree are tied to some thought or idea that is contrary to the Word of God. It is like a chain reaction. We don't feel free, so we don't act free. Our actions are based on our emotions, which are based on our thinking. Our souls are made up of our minds, our emotions, and our wills. The Word of God should control our thoughts and pour over into our emotions. But we don't feel free because our emotions are controlled by our thinking and our thinking is not in line with the Word of God. The world is in bondage to sin and does not walk according to God's Word. If we think the way the world thinks and walk the way the world walks, it will be impossible for us to think the way God thinks and walk in the freedom Christ has for us.

Proverbs 23:7 (KJV) says that as a man thinks in his heart, so is he. Whatever he is deep inside spills out into his actions and lifestyle. So, if inside of you are the beliefs, "I can't," or "I'm afraid," or "I don't know," then that is what will come out. Jesus Himself said in Matthew 12:34b that "out of the overflow of the heart the mouth speaks." You don't have to be with people very long before you know where they are coming from. You will hear their love or their criticism; their complaining and fears; their doubts and hang-ups. Out of the overflow of the heart come the issues of life.

We will not be able to walk in freedom until we change our thinking. This is true for churches as well as for individuals. Thousands of churches are bound up in negativism and defeat and not walking in the freedom of Christ. Changing our thinking is not simply a matter of pulling ourselves up by our own bootstraps and choosing to think nice thoughts. It's not that simple. We need to have our minds renewed and we need to be transformed from conforming to the world so we can see who we really are in Christ.

Free in Christ!

How do you see yourself? What is the "real" you? Do you see yourself as a son or daughter of God, born into a royal family, created for a royal purpose, and heir to a royal kingdom? That's how God sees you. You and I and all Christians need to learn to see ourselves as the Lord sees us and walk accordingly. How else does God see you?

You are a totally and intensely loved person who has been rescued from satan's realm of spiritual death and dominion of darkness, and brought into the Kingdom of God's own dear Son, Jesus (see Col. 1:13). He has given you eternal life and fellowship and union with Him. You have been spiritually reborn, created anew by the ever-powerful and ever-living Word of God. You are a completely new creature united as one spirit with Jesus Christ, separated totally from all the sin and hindrances of the past (see 1 Cor. 6:17; 2 Cor. 5:17). The same Spirit that raised Him from the dead lives in you, and you are now a joint heir with Jesus (see Rom. 8:11; Gal. 4:7). He has given you His ability, potential, and strength to be victorious in every situation; to be prosperous and be in health even as your soul is prospering (see 3 Jn. 2). You are stamped with the seal of ownership of the Holy Spirit and are filled with His power (see 2 Cor. 1:22). He is able to do within you far more than you could ever ask or think, enabling you to be a co-worker with God, witnessing of His love in word and deed, doing mighty signs and wonders, and being a channel of His healing and restoration in the name of Jesus (see Eph. 3:20). He has given you power and authority over satan and his schemes so you are able to resist him and stand firm in your faith (see Lk. 9:1; Jas. 4:7).

Shining like a star in a dark world before non-believers, you can hold out to and offer to all men the word of life. In your new life in Christ you can stand firm and strong, single-minded and in constant fellowship with your Christian brothers and sisters and with your heavenly Father. You have been loved, planned for, known, chosen, and called from before the foundation of the world, and blessed in Christ with every spiritual blessing (see Eph. 1:3). You are part of a chosen race, a royal priesthood, a holy nation declaring His

wonderful works, bearing good fruit, and being changed
more and more into the image and likeness of Jesus (see
1 Pet. 2:9).

Wow! As Paul writes, "What, then, shall we say in response to this? If God is for us, who can be against us?"
(Rom. 8:31) Jesus Himself continually intercedes for us,
and nothing, absolutely nothing, can separate us from the
love of God in Christ Jesus (see Rom. 8:35-39). Once we allow the Holy Spirit to open our eyes to understand this, we
will never again have the same attitude toward ourselves. It
will be impossible. When we understand who we are in
Christ, we will want absolutely nothing else but to be in the
very center of His will. We won't be able to imagine being
anywhere else. It will be like a love affair that just keeps
growing and growing and growing.

Knowing who we are in Jesus will knock us out of our
spiritual complacency. There are so many in the Body of
Christ who are satisfied with things as they are and have become lukewarm. We know from Revelation 3:15-16 that
God would rather have us hot or cold. At least then He can
do something with us. If we are lukewarm He wants to spit
us out of His mouth.

Jesus came to give us abundant life. That abundance is
rooted in spiritual freedom. The reality of that freedom
needs to become deeply planted within us so that we can
move on to greater maturity and usefulness. So many Christians never seem to get past their initial salvation experience or their baptism of the Holy Spirit. They never
move on to walking in victory and in healing and wholeness, or to become catalysts through whom the life of God
is released into the world.

Paul stated wonderfully well in Philippians 3:12-14 the
importance of moving on:

I'm not saying that I have this all together, that I have it made. But I am well on my way, reaching out for Christ, who has so wondrously reached out for me. Friends, don't get me wrong: By no means do I count myself an expert in all of this, but I've got my eye on the goal, where God is beckoning us onward—to Jesus. I'm off and running, and I'm not turning back (Philippians 3:12-14, The Message).

Abiding in the Word

The basis of our freedom in Christ is found in John 8:31-32, 36:

...If you abide in My word [hold fast to My teachings and live in accordance with them], you are truly My disciples. And you will know the Truth, and the Truth will set you free. ... So if the Son liberates you [makes you free men], then you are really and unquestionably free (AMP).

First of all, the basis of our freedom is to abide in the words or the teachings of Jesus. He said the truth would set us free. His Word is truth. Knowledge of His Word, therefore, brings freedom. Abiding in the Word is much deeper than simply reading or hearing it. Essentially, it means to stay or remain permanently in, dwell in, live in, and continue on in. Abiding is not so much an act we perform as it is a position we occupy.

Abiding also means being "vitally united to." I am a former nurse by profession, and when I worked in the hospital one of my regular responsibilities was to check patients' vital signs: temperature, pulse, respiration, blood pressure, etc. **Vital** means essential for life. Vital signs were those indicators whose presence were indispensable for life. I loved it when I discovered that to abide means to be vitally united to. It is a spiritual vital sign, indispensable for spiritual life. Abiding is a consistent, continual dwelling in His Word and allowing it to dwell in us. It means letting the Word of God be the basis for all we think about God, about life, about ourselves, about others, about our plans, and about our walk with Him. Just as we need oxygen to survive physically, so we need the supernatural oxygen of the Word of God continually flowing through us. Then we, as Christians, can live life with a capital "L".

John 8:31-32 contains a specific promise related to abiding: If we abide in Christ's word, we will know the truth. That word **know** is interesting. The Greek term, *ginosko*, means not simply intellectual or head knowledge, but a total involvement of the entire person. The same word is used elsewhere in the Scriptures to describe sexual union between a husband and wife. It means deep, intimate, personal knowledge; a oneness of mind, heart, will, and body.

The same Greek word is used in John 17:3 when Jesus prays to the Father, "...that they may **know** You, the only true God, and Jesus Christ, whom You have sent." That's a knowing deep in your gut, a knowing so deep that no circumstance of life can change it. Knowing the truth that intimately is a liberating reality, but it will come only from the position of abiding.

Lloyd John Ogilvie reminds us that since the Word of God is true, and since it says that the Son, who is Truth, shall make us free, then anything that makes us feel unfree must be tied to some thought or perception that is contrary to the Word of God.

All of us have our own ideas and opinions about God and His ways. Many of them come from legalistic backgrounds and traditions. Some of them may even come from pharisaical spirits that would blind us to the truth of God's liberating love. The enemy does not want us to know who we are in Christ. He doesn't want us to understand the covenant relationship we have with God or the miracle of our new birth, so he tries to blind us with legalism, rules, and regulations that keep us from moving out as spiritual sons and daughters of God.

God does have a hand in our lives. He has a purpose and plan and is fully able to complete what He started. Somehow, the Church has come out with the idea that we totally determine our destiny in God. Where is God in this? I heard a pastor say once that the sooner we realize that God is God and we are not, the better we will be. Romans 8:28-29 says:

> *And we know that in all things God works for the good of those who love Him, who have been called according to His purpose. For those God foreknew He also predestined to be conformed to the likeness of His Son, that He might be the firstborn among many brothers.*

All of Romans chapter 8 deals with being changed into spiritual men and women, that is glorious, mature, "sons" of God. These verses say that in all of our circumstances, God is working to fulfill His purpose of conforming us, His children, into the very likeness of Jesus. We are being conformed into the image of Christ, not only to show forth His power and His abilities, but also to manifest His very nature on earth.

The Word of God is true. It also has the power within it to change our lives. First Thessalonians 2:13 in the Amplified Bible says:

And we also [especially] thank God continually for this, that when you received the message of God [which you heard] from us, you welcomed it not as the word of [mere] men, but as it truly is, the Word of God, which is effectually at work in you who believe [exercising its superhuman power in those who adhere to and trust in and rely on it] (1 Thessalonians 2:13 AMP).

God's power changes us as we abide in His Word. The Holy Spirit works through the Word to make us more and more like Jesus.

Meditating on the Word

How on earth does God's Word change us and bring into reality the freedom we desire? It happens as we establish habitual patterns of hearing and thinking the truth. This is where our free choice comes into play. I have said many times that faith comes by hearing and hearing and hearing the Word of God (see Rom. 10:17). It comes from talking about it and fixing our minds on it. Most of us ponder everything under the sun except the things of God. We fix our minds, daily, on things that bring us into a state of unbelief and lack of freedom. We ponder the problems, the fear, the self-consciousness, the disappointments, the frustrations, and the sickness. God tells us to fix our minds on Him, on His Word, and on His truth, and He will change us.

This Book of the Law shall not depart out of your mouth, but you shall meditate on it day and night, that you may observe and do according to all that is written in it. For then you shall make your way prosperous, and then you shall deal wisely and have good success (Joshua 1:8 AMP).

Moses was dead. Joshua was poised to lead the Israelites into the Promised Land. The Lord spoke to Joshua and told him to meditate on His Word. That is another way of saying Joshua was to fix his mind on it. There is life in the Word of God. It is not a book of rules and regulations, despite what many Christians have made it over the years. It is a love book; it is God's expression of covenant love to His sons and daughters. Meditating on God's love book will make an awesome difference in our lives.

The Hebrew word for "meditate" denotes an active recitation, a speaking, of God's words. That's what the Lord meant when He told Joshua that His words should not depart from his mouth. Meditating on the Word builds our capacity for deeper faith. When we meditate on His Word, we take it deep into our hearts, gain insight from it, and establish a greater understanding of God and His ways.

Christian meditation means to ponder God's Word, to think on it, to dwell on and contemplate it. We can meditate on the Word wherever we are. I think many Christians who try this meet with limited success because they try to ingest too much of the Word at one time. Following a Bible reading plan is fine if you want to get a good overview of the Scriptures and its teachings. Bible study, with its dictionaries and commentaries and word studies, is essential when preparing to teach, or for personal growth and discipline. Meditation is different.

When we meditate, we take a small portion of Scripture, just a verse or two, and chew on it. We turn it around, look at it from every angle, and just feed on it. The more we fix our minds on it and the more we contemplate it, the more its meaning opens up for us and the more life it possesses. The Holy Spirit brings the living Word of God to life for us and in us. In this way we feed our spirit man with food necessary for growth.

I remember when the Spirit truly captured my heart with the vitality of the Word. For three months He kept me in the first three chapters of Ephesians. I wrestled with the words and promises there about the blessings of God, the inheritance of the saints, my hope in Christ, and the greatness of His power in me. Gradually, as I pondered and contemplated, I began to grasp something of the truths of being "in Christ."

Wonderful things happen when we take God's Word and begin to meditate on it. It starts to become constant in our thoughts and in our mouths, and He speaks to our hearts through it. Second Timothy 3:16-17 in the Amplified Bible says:

Every Scripture is God-breathed (given by His inspiration) and profitable for instruction, for reproof and conviction of sin, for correction of error and discipline in obedience, [and] for training in righteousness (in holy living, in conformity to God's will in thought, purpose, and action), so that the man of God may be complete and proficient, well fitted and thoroughly equipped for every good work.

This is the basis for life and for freedom—the Word of God. Meditate on it. Plant it in you until it becomes second nature for you. Move in it, walk in it, and apply it to reality. It will change your heart and mind. The Word of God is your surest source of guidance for hearing the voice of God.

Dr. Billy Graham said one time that if he had it to do over again he would spend more time meditating on God's Word to hear God speak to him, rather than praying and talking to God all the time. It is difficult to overestimate the importance of meditation for our spiritual nourishment and growth.

Psalm 1 contains some beautiful promises for those who meditate on the Word of God. Look at Psalm 1:2-3 from the Amplified Bible:

But his delight and desire are in the law of the Lord, and on His law (the precepts, the instructions, the teachings of God) he habitually meditates (ponders and studies) by day and by night. And he shall be like a tree firmly planted [and tended] by the streams of water, ready to bring forth its fruit in its season; its leaf also shall not fade or wither; and everything he does shall prosper [and come to maturity].

One of the promises is that we shall prosper. Biblical prosperity means success in what we put our hands to, to do. God wants us to be successful. He wants us to be fruitful. To be prosperous means to be successful and continually fruitful, not dead on the limb. The Word of God has the power to make us prosper.

Another promise is that we will be like a tree firmly planted by streams of water and producing consistent, good fruit. God has a way of keeping us in unity and oneness with Him that will bring life and fruitfulness, and solidly ground us in the faith. We need to be firmly grounded because there are winds of false doctrine blowing all the time. If we are solidly grounded in our faith and in the Word, we will not be tossed aside or bent out of shape with everything that blows our way.

A third promise is that we will not fade or wither. We will not become spiritually dry. I know that we all go through dry times, but the promise is that if we meditate on the Word and it is grafted in our hearts, then deep inside, His well still fills and refreshes us, producing prosperity and success in life.

Jeremiah 17:7-8 contains a similar promise:

[Most] blessed is the man who believes in, trusts in, and relies on the Lord, and whose hope and confidence the Lord is. For he shall be like a tree planted by the waters that spreads out its roots by the river; and it shall not see and fear when heat comes; but its leaf shall be green. It shall not be anxious and full of care in a year of drought, nor shall it cease yielding fruit (AMP).

Some of us have been in a dry and thirsty land for a long time. If God's Word is so engrafted in us, if His river is flowing deep within us, then we will not be anxious or full of care; even in the midst of drought we will continue to bear fruit.

None of us are on our own to bring all this about. God gives us the power to think His thoughts and to do His will. That's the progression: thinking right then acting right. When our minds are transformed, out of that metamorphosis will flow the actions of life. When we **know** we are free, we will **feel** free; and when we **feel** free, we will **act** free.

Jesus Christ bought our freedom with His own blood. Even though we are free in Him, we still belong to Him. We are born free, yet at the same time we enjoy an exalted status—we are His very own, very special possession.

Chapter 4

Our Status–His Possession

A number of years ago I had a vision that changed forever my perception of who I am in Christ. In this vision I was standing in a huge cathedral that had stone floors, wide pews, a wide center aisle, and massive columns that rose next to the outside walls. Beautiful arched windows were set into the walls. At the back of the room, immense double doors stood tightly closed. At the far end, brilliant light radiated from a throne sitting on a raised, stepped platform. A figure stood on the platform. It was Jesus.

The double doors opened and a timid little creature peeked around. It was me. I crept in, went to the side, and made my way silently from pillar to pillar, sneaking my way to the front. When I reached the platform I groveled on my hands and knees, hoping against hope that the One on the throne would receive me.

Instantly, the scene changed. It was the same room, the same throne, the same brilliant light, and the same Jesus. There were even the same double doors at the back. This time, though, the doors opened wide and I stood in the center of the doorway. All of a sudden, as fast as I could run, I flew down that aisle, up those steps, and right into the arms of the One who sat on the throne.

It is a picture I will never forget. No matter what circumstance I am in, I know I can always zoom right into God's presence, right into His arms. He's my **Abba**, my Daddy.

Which of these scenes best describes your perception of where you stand with God?

Saved and Sure

Do you remember when you received Christ as your Savior? There are many different ways to describe that event. Perhaps you prefer to say you were converted. Jesus used the term **born again**, which really describes in a wonderful way what happened to all of us when we first came to Him. Can you recall when that transaction took place? You may have been very young and do not remember the exact time or circumstances. Or you may have come to Him in the midst of tremendous pain, challenge, or turmoil. You may have been grabbed by an anointed message at church and turned to the living Christ rather than formal religion. Whatever your personal experience may be and however you choose to describe it, if you are a Christian, then there was a time in your life when, of your own free will and volition, you embraced Jesus. There was a time when Jesus became more than just a name to you; He became real to you for the first time.

Do you know that you know that you know that you are a child of God? Are you sure that when you leave your body you will go to Heaven? Someone may say, "I hope so, but how can I know for sure? How can anyone know for sure?" First John 5:13 says, "I write these things to you who believe in the name of the Son of God so that you may **know** that you have eternal life." There should be no doubt at all. Jesus is our hope, and He wants us to know that we have eternal life. Biblical hope is not a "maybe" kind of thing, but a confidence based on rock-solid certainty. If we are in Christ, then our salvation is not a "I hope so" matter. It is a sure thing.

Romans 3:22a says, "This righteousness from God comes through faith in Jesus Christ to all who believe." It has nothing to do with feelings or appearances. Our feelings change with the weather. If they were my guidelines for whether or not I was right with God, half the time I wouldn't know whether I was in or out. Our right standing with God is a fact. Christ within us is a fact. The anointing of the Holy Spirit within us is a fact. Our place in Him is based on what His Word says, not on what our emotions say. There is no such thing as being a little bit pregnant. There is no such thing as being a little alive or a little dead. You either are or you aren't. It is either one or the other. Likewise, there is no such thing as being a little righteous. You either are or you aren't. It is as simple as that.

In certain Christian circles there is a definite "God is going to get you" doctrine that produces legalism and defeat. Those caught up in it are led to believe that they can never measure up to or attain God's standards, and are in constant danger of losing their salvation. Like all legalism, this is sin. It is not resting in the finished work of Jesus, but adding to what was accomplished on the cross. I firmly believe that we don't jump in and out of our relationship with Him. Too often we jump in and out of fellowship, but that is different. We have a relationship with God by virtue of the Lord Jesus Christ giving us the miracle of the new birth. We are His children. That will never change. We can allow our fellowship with Him to be broken, however. Fellowship has to do with our walk and our intimacy. Fellowship varies; relationship is fixed. Even when we don't walk closely with God, which surely grieves Him, we are still His children.

This is significant because it relates to the whole concept of our releasing life into the Body of Christ and to a lost world. We must have life to release it, and we cannot release it effectively unless we are confident and secure in our position in Christ.

We can be secure in that position because when we came to Christ we were not only set free, but we also were established as His very own and very special possessions.

Prized Possessions

Think about the word **possession**. What does it mean? A possession is something you own, either because you purchased it or because it was given to you as a gift. It is something that belongs to you and is yours to do with as you please. Both aspects of the word are important in our Christian walk. We possess eternal life because God gave it to us as a gift. We belong to Christ because He purchased us with His blood.

We are His magnificent possessions. In His love He chose us. He picked us out for Himself as His very own before the foundation of the world. We are set apart for Him, holy and blameless in His sight. In Him we already have redemption, deliverance, forgiveness of sins, and salvation through His blood. (See Ephesians 1:4,7.) He has rescued us out of the darkness and gloom of satan's kingdom and brought us into the glorious light of His own Kingdom (see Col. 1:13). Our bodies are temples of the Holy Spirit who lives in us and whom we have received as His gift. We are not our own, but were bought for a price and paid for, and we belong to Him. (See 1 Corinthians 6:19-20.)

God is passionate about that which is His. We are His and He is passionate about us. Don't you think God has the right to love, redeem, deliver, restore, hold on to, and care for those whom He has purchased? God is God, and what He says He will do, He will do. He has a purpose and a plan for us that He is quite able to carry out.

Because we are in Christ, born again of the Spirit of God, we are completely new creatures. The old life, all that we were before Christ, has passed away, and a new spiritual life, fresh and vital, has come. God's life, *zoe*, has been imparted to us. It fills us and overflows from us. We are different individuals now than we were before we became Christians. Because of our new birth in Christ, we can right now come boldly into God's presence with no guilt, condemnation, or inferiority (see Heb. 4:16 KJV).

When will the Church as a whole come to understand this truth and walk in it? Jesus did not come to patch up the old and make us acceptable, but to make us totally new. He came to give us abundant life.

First Corinthians 6:17 says, "But he who unites himself with the Lord is one with Him in spirit." How often do you think of yourself as being "one with Him"? *One* means a unity, inseparable. We are inseparably part of Christ. That's what the Word says.

First Corinthians 1:30 says, "It is because of [God] that you are in Christ Jesus, who has become for us wisdom from God—that is, our righteousness, holiness and redemption." God imparts His life to us through Jesus Christ. We share in His wisdom, righteousness, holiness, and redemption. We are partakers of His nature. Those things are ours no matter how unrighteous or unholy or unworthy we may feel at times. What God has done in us is absolutely tremendous.

Two words in particular in this verse call for further consideration: **righteousness** and **holiness**.

Righteous in Christ

Are you righteous? Whenever I ask that question at a conference or a study session I get a wide variety of answers. Some people say no; others say yes. Most answers fall somewhere in between: "Righteous, yes, but...." How about you? One woman said that righteousness is something God does through the blood of Jesus, but was a process she was growing in.

In short, the answer is yes. We are righteous. As believers we have been given the righteousness of Christ. Most of us feel awkward talking about our own righteousness because we are afraid that it will sound like we are boasting. I think part of the problem stems from the fact that many Christians do not understand the difference between righteousness and holiness.

Righteousness literally means a right standing with God. It is a relational position of being perfectly acceptable in His sight with no barriers or hindrances of any kind separating us from Him. Righteousness is an instantaneous act of God's grace imparted to us the moment we believe. As soon as we receive Christ, the old, unholy, unrighteous sin nature passes away, and a new spiritual nature of righteousness and holiness is born.

How can that be? Don't we still struggle daily with sin in our lives, thoughts, attitudes, and behavior? We certainly do. Apart from Christ we have no righteousness. Isaiah 64:6

says that "all our righteous acts are like filthy rags." None of us are righteous on our own, nor can we ever be. This has nothing to do with being goody-goody, acting right, being nice and kind, or loving and benevolent. You could be the biggest philanthropist the world has ever seen and send millions to Africa. You could pour out food to the hungry or funds to your church. You could build hospitals. You could give and give and give, doing everything wonderful and good under the sun, but without God in your life it would all mean nothing. It would be as filthy rags.

This is one of the hardest things for people to understand. We look at outward appearances; God looks at the heart. If the things we do, no matter how good they are, do not come from the divine life within us, then they are of the flesh and are as filthy rags in God's eyes.

If we have no righteousness of our own, and yet as believers are righteous in God's eyes, where does our righteousness come from? Look again at First Corinthians 1:30. Jesus Christ "has become for us…our righteousness…." **Our righteousness comes from Jesus. It is His, not ours. He is our righteousness.**

I had a good friend who was very active in her church. With her big, compassionate, caring heart she was like a mama bear. She served on the board of elders but also brought in the lonely, the hungry, and the rejected. She loved them all. Somewhere in her thirties she realized that she had never come into a living relationship with Jesus Christ. "I never loved until Jesus," she told me. She understood the difference.

Righteousness is something we were given when we were born again, not something we attain by our own efforts. Romans 5:15-17 makes this clear:

> But the *gift is not like the trespass. For if the many died by the trespass of the one man, how much more did God's grace and the **gift** that came by the grace of the one man, Jesus Christ, overflow to the many! Again, the **gift** of God is not like the result of the one man's sin: The judgment followed one sin and brought condemnation, but the **gift** followed many trespasses and brought justification. For if, by the trespass of the one man, death reigned through that one man, how much more will those who receive God's abundant provision of grace and of the **gift** of righteousness reign in life through the one man, Jesus Christ* (Romans 5:15-17).

The phrase "the gift" occurs five times in those three verses. The gift comes from the grace of God. It brings **justification**. It is the gift of righteousness. Justification is a word that means God has declared us not guilty, just as if we had never sinned.

Righteousness is a free gift that comes to us with our faith in Christ and His finished work on the cross. Sometimes we cry out to Jesus to do this and to do that for us. Listen. He's already done it all for us. He completed it 2,000 years ago on the cross. When He said "It is finished," He meant "It is finished!" Now He wants us to move out as sons and daughters of God in the righteousness He has given us using all the resources He has made available to us.

Holy in Christ

One of the fruits of righteousness is a life of holiness. Whereas righteousness is instantaneous, holiness is a process. The proper theological or scriptural word is **sanctification**, or being set apart for God's use and glory. It is a process of growth. Holiness is living in such a way that the life of Jesus becomes more and more evident and observable in us. Our lives begin to display more and more the fruit of the Spirit: love, joy, peace, patience, kindness, goodness, faithfulness, gentleness, and self-control (see Gal. 5:22-23).

Holiness is something we work out in day-to-day experience. It is what Paul had in mind when he wrote, "...continue to work out your salvation with fear and trembling" (Phil. 2:12). This does not mean we are left to carry on in our own strength. It means we are to recognize our weaknesses and learn more and more to depend completely on the Lord to produce His life and His nature in us. That's why Paul continues on to say, "For it is God who works in you to will and to act according to His good purpose" (Phil. 2:13). We depend on Him and He produces the fruit of righteousness, a life of holiness, in us.

When will we break free of the mentality that says, "Thank You, God. You saved me and now I've got to make it work from now until I see You face-to-face"? Salvation is by grace through faith (see Eph. 2:8). Spirituality is by grace through faith. It is all the work of God, not at all the work of man. Our part is to make ourselves available to Him and to be willing to let Him mold us into His likeness.

Do you realize that holiness lives within you, that it has already been implanted in your spirit? It's Him. It's His nature. He is the Holy One. He is the Righteous One. I really believe that when we grasp the truth about our righteousness with God, we will have fewer and fewer problems moving in holiness.

Romans 6:19 says that righteousness leads to holiness. The problem is that many of us come from a background that says we must get this cleaned up, get that straightened out, make this right, fix that, etc., and then we will be holy and righteous. Paul said, "...live by the Spirit, and you will not gratify the desires of the sinful nature" (Gal. 5:16).God wants us to see ourselves as so accepted and beloved by Him that we will respond as sons and daughters rather than as slaves.

It is really a cooperative effort. At the new birth our spirit is completely reborn by the Spirit of God, who then desires to transform our soul, that is, our mind, will and emotions. It is our responsibility to take His Word and let it renew our minds, and to place it deep within our hearts where it can take control of our choices and actions in everyday life.

The Ties That Bind

Despite the greatness of these truths of our righteousness and holiness, as well as our security in Christ, there are still many Christians who do not walk in the awareness of them. This is due to any of several reasons. One is legalism. When churches or denominations focus on rules and restrictions, forms and traditions, and judgmental spirits to make people toe the line, then the entire concept of freedom, security, joy, and wholeness in the Lord is buried. The "law of sin and death" (Rom. 8:2) is replaced by another restrictive man-made system that is just as deadly.

Another tie that binds is ignorance. We are brand-new in Christ and totally free, yet so many of us don't see ourselves that way. All we see is the awful struggle that we face every day to simply cope. The enemy wants to keep us in ignorance. He doesn't want us to know who we are, or what resources are available to us. Paul told the Corinthians that he did not want them to be ignorant of the things of the Spirit of God (see 1 Cor. 12:1). Ignorant doesn't mean stupid, but untaught and unlearned. The problem is that many of us in the Church are so ignorant of our righteousness and freedom in Christ that all we have is a deep sin-consciousness and a sense of failure. We need to be released into a deep consciousness of our righteousness—a righteousness awareness. Once we do this, the result will be right living.

Another limitation is false humility. Many of us face defeat, failure, or lack of fruit in our spiritual lives and so try to compensate by adopting a self-debasing attitude. We say, "Righteous? Who, me? That can't be. Not me. I'm too weak. I'm too sinful. I can never be righteous." I don't think we should ever talk that way. It is one thing to recognize our weaknesses, but it is quite another to dismiss the life-changing power of God in us. If we have been made the righteousness of God in Christ and are in right standing with Him, then how can we "humbly" say, "I'm just an old sinner saved by grace"? Although it certainly is true that we are saved by grace, we are not "just" old sinners; we are new creatures. We are saints. We are blood-bought sons and daughters of God. Let us stop confessing with false humility that we are no more than dirty old sinners. The Word of God tells us that we have been rescued from that.

A fourth binding tie is a "worm" mentality. Some Christians come from a background that has taught them that they are filthy, no-good "worms" unworthy of God's attention. This is a very debilitating mind-set that makes it difficult to believe and accept the liberating truth of the righteousness of God in Christ that has been imparted to us. Jesus Christ did not die for worms. He died for creatures of infinite worth, people created in the image of God, to transform them into sons and daughters of Almighty God, children who would bear the stamp of His life in them.

We are children of God and have eternal life right now as a present reality. We are daily working out our salvation, growing into a life of holiness, as we face the challenges of daily living. This is the difference between positional truth and temporal truth. Positionally, we are righteous before God now and forever. Temporally, we still struggle with sin and our sinful nature while we are being conformed into the image of Christ. Our problems with temptation and sin come because we fail to recognize the attempts of our flesh to rule over us. Paul tells us to consider ourselves dead to them (see Rom. 6:1-11). It is a daily challenge. God is faithful, however, and will complete the work He has begun in each of us (see Phil. 1:6).

Some Christians fear that such an emphasis on freedom in Christ could lead to a license to sin. Such a fear fails to account for the powerful influence of the new spiritual nature present in all believers. According to Galatians 5:16 we are to live by the Spirit and not gratify the desires of the sinful nature. In Romans chapter 7 Paul describes in a very personal way the struggle of the natural man against the spiritual man. He says that the things he wants to do are not the things he does, and the things he does are the things he does not want to do. What a dilemma. No wonder Paul says, "Woe is me!" He goes on to praise God for the deliverance he has received in Christ Jesus. There is now no condemnation. Romans chapter 8 moves from the struggle of the natural man to the formation of mature **sons** of God (includes both male and female), learning to walk not after the things of the flesh, but after the things of the Spirit. Our new godly nature fills us with godly desires, and the power of the Spirit enables us to fulfill them.

Look at the parable of the prodigal son (see Lk. 15:11-32). The young man was always a son. Even if he had never come back home, he was still a son. The father saw him, from a long way off, coming home. I think he saw the boy with the eyes of faith and revelation. The father ran to meet his son while he was still a long way from home. That father's compassion for his son is just like our heavenly Father's for you and me during those times when we have been a long way off.

What did the father do with his son, that smelly, dirty, gaunt, scruffy, bare-footed rebel? The father put shoes on his feet, a glorious robe on his back, and a ring on his finger. Then they went home for a big party in celebration of the son's return. The only one who had the problem was the elder brother who said, "He took off on you. I've been here working for you all these years and you never gave me a thing." The father replied, "It has been here for you all along. All you had to do was take it. It's yours."

The same is true for us. All the wealth and resources of the Father are ours because we are His children. He has given us the gift of righteousness through His Son, Jesus Christ, who bought us with His own blood.

When we meet God face to face one day, none of us will be any more righteous than we are right now. Righteousness is a state that He has brought us into, and He keeps us there. A popular phrase in recent years has been, "Please be patient, God isn't finished with me yet." That is true in the temporal realm, but not in the spiritual. Jesus finished with us spiritually 2,000 years ago, at least where our relational position in Him is concerned. Recognizing our place in God is not a position of pride, but one from which fruit will grow. One vitally important fruit that will grow from our positioning as righteous children of God is a walk of intimacy and abiding in Him.

Chapter 5

Close Encounters
of the Best Kind

During high school I had a terrible crush on this guy. I couldn't get him out of my mind or out of my heart. I'd do almost anything to get his attention. He lived about six blocks up the street from me. My second-floor bedroom had a big bay window with a wide curved seat and after I got ready for school, I would scrunch myself up on the window seat, press my nose against the window, and watch for him. From that position I could see between the trees and about five houses up. I had it all arranged. As soon as his legs appeared I would grab my books and rush out the door and up to the corner, saying, "Hi! Oh, you're walking this way too?" I did this all the time just so I could walk with him, but he never really gave me the time of day.

Later, while he was in medical school and I was still in high school, and after he had broken up with his girlfriend, he threw me some crumbs for a year, inviting me to football games and dances and such. Nothing ever came of it, but how well I remember the feelings I had for him—the desire simply to be in his presence, to hear his voice on the phone or talk with him in the hall, to catch his eye, or his smile— just the longing and hunger for his company.

A few years ago, while preparing to move to a new home, I found stashed away in a shoe box some priceless love letters exchanged between me and my husband Bill over the four years prior to our marriage. There was even one I had written to my mom, which she had saved, telling her that I had found the man I wanted to marry and how I felt about him. They were wonderfully "mushy," well-handled and creased in the folds from being read countless times. They expressed our deep longing for each other.

Have you ever had a longing like that to be in the presence of the Lord? Would you ever think of moving into an ongoing, satisfying, ever deepening love affair with Him? Could you consider Him as the initiator, the aggressor, and the winner of your heart? Do you ever think of Him that way? Do you ever hunger and long just for His close presence, or is He the Father, Son, and Holy Spirit, but still way out there somewhere?

Intimacy With Christ

The subject of this chapter is intimacy. Have you ever thought much about being intimate with the Lord Jesus Christ? I mean spending time with Him and getting to know Him in a deeply personal way. The word *intimacy* means a close personal relationship, a warm friendship. It is very private, deeply cherished, and familiar. Is such a relationship with Jesus actually possible?

Intimacy with Jesus is the missing ingredient to the move of the Holy Spirit in our churches. I believe that is true no matter which group or denomination we are from.

Whether in our personal lives or in our corporate experience in our churches, we miss this intimacy basically for two reasons.

First, we do not prepare ahead of time to meet with Him. We zip right into a worship service or Bible study or some other meeting with all sorts of things on our minds, and expect Him to simply show up and perform. We do not take time to prepare our hearts through prayer or praise or quiet meditation. There is no time for that. We are too busy. "Just fill us, Lord. Anoint us so we can minister. Thank You." Then we wonder why we are disappointed so often.

Too many times we are interested more in what we want than in what He wants. One day I was sitting before Him, curled up in a chair in a small room in my house. I had some important work ahead of me or something, and I needed to plan. I was getting myself prepared. All of a sudden I felt the Lord say to me very clearly, "The only reason you really want to have this time with Me is because you want Me to do something."

In other words, my motive was rather stinky. I wanted to be in an intimate place with Him so that I could have all the ingredients I needed to go out and be a fruitful minister. He wants us to seek His face, not just His hand, and too often we're satisfied with just His hand.

The second reason we miss intimacy with Christ is because we do not walk and fellowship with Him consistently. We wait until a crisis comes before we call on Him. I like how one writer put it:

> "God is called by many names. He is the Lord our Healer, our Provider, our Banner, and our Righteousness. He also promises to be our Deliverer. In this

troubled world that may very well be what we need Him to be most often.

"But there are many believers who never experience God's mighty delivering power because, instead of walking closely with Him day by day, they wait until danger strikes to call upon Him. That just doesn't work. If you want God to rescue you in the bad times, you have to fellowship with Him in the good times. Why? Because God responds to faith. Our faith, not our need, is what causes Him to act on our behalf. And we'll never begin to be able to develop that kind of faith, that kind of trust and confidence in Him, if we don't spend enough time with Him to get to know Him."[1]

Isn't that true? We wait until disaster strikes, then scurry around trying to find the thing that will heal instead of walking in an ever-increasing day-by-day abiding in Christ. No matter how needy we are, it is our faith, not our need, that will move God to answer us.

Intimacy speaks of close union, of tight love. In First Corinthians 6:17 Paul says, "But he who unites himself with the Lord is one with Him in spirit." We are linked as one with the Lord Jesus Christ. When that fact begins to sink in, it will make a difference in our approach to Him, ourselves, and our ministries. Don't let anyone criticize you or put you down because you desire an experience with Almighty God.

Consider Paul's words to the Ephesian church in chapter 3. He writes: "...May you be rooted deep in love and founded securely on love, that you may have the power and be strong to apprehend and grasp with all the saints [God's devoted people, the **experience** of that love] what is the breadth and length and height and depth [of it]; [that you may really come] to know [practically, through **experience** for yourselves] the love of Christ, which far surpasses mere knowledge [without **experience**]…" (Eph. 3:17-19 AMP)

There is an old hymn that expresses beautifully this warm intimacy with Jesus:

> I've found a friend, O such a friend!
> He loved me ere I knew Him;
> He drew me with the cords of love,
> And thus He bound me to Him;
> And round my heart, still closely twine
> Those ties which naught can sever,
> For I am His, and Christ is mine,
> Forever and forever.
>
> I've found a friend, O such a friend!
> He bled, He died to save me;
> And not alone the gift of life,
> But His own self He gave me;
> Naught that I have my own I call,
> I hold it for the Giver;
> My heart, my strength, my life, my all
> Are His, and His forever.
>
> I've found a friend, O such a friend!
> All power to Him is given,
> To guard me on my onward course,
> And bring me safe to heaven:
> The eternal glories gleam afar
> To nerve my faint endeavor;
> So now to watch, to work, to war,
> And then to rest forever.

I've found a friend, O such a friend,
So kind and true and tender,
So wise a counselor and guide,
So mighty a defender!
From Him who loves me now so well
What power my soul can sever?
Shall life or death or earth or hell?
No, I am His forever.[2]

Abiding in Christ

The first thing that Jesus said when He called His disciples was, "Come, follow Me." They came from everywhere, from all walks of life, men and women, and they came for many different reasons. For some it was curiosity; for others, a desire for a change of pace. Some came out of love and a desire for the deeper things of God. Mostly, though, whether or not they realized it at the time, they came because they were drawn by the Holy Spirit.

Following Jesus was the first step for these disciples. Not yet spiritual people, they followed in the flesh, initially. They spent time with Jesus, watching, listening, and learning. In time, Jesus began to draw them deeper. He shared with them such things as, "Trust in Me, learn of Me, hear My words." He even trained them to imitate His works and sent them out to preach, heal, and cast out demons. Such growth came because of their fellowship, familiarity, and communication with Him.

The pattern we see in the Gospels is one of Jesus bringing His disciples from an initial superficial attachment to a growing intimacy with Him. He led them from following to abiding. As the day of His death approached, Jesus concentrated on preparing His disciples for His departure. After He was gone, they would no longer be able to follow Him physically; they would have to **abide in Him**.

Abiding in Christ is a work of the Spirit; it cannot be accomplished in the flesh. I think most of us are in that place of learning to trust Jesus, learn of Him, and hear His words. He wants us to do more than just follow Him, however. He has called us to abide in Him. Much of what we do to serve Him and please Him is done in the flesh because we do not understand this abiding in Him. We experience disappointment, defeat, and fruitlessness because we do not grasp the reality of abiding in Him. We need to become spiritual men and women abiding in Christ, walking in the Spirit, and following His agenda, not ours.

Jesus' teaching on abiding is found in chapter 15 of John. It is a vital chapter on positioning and intimacy, found in the middle of a five-chapter record of His deeper teachings to the disciples. In chapter 13 He teaches them about the importance of the servant's heart. Chapters 14 and 16 tell of the coming and the ministry of the Holy Spirit, while chapter 17 records Jesus' great intercessory prayer for all His followers.

Here is what Jesus said about abiding:

I am the True Vine, and My Father is the Vinedresser. Any branch in Me that does not bear fruit [that stops bearing] He cuts away (trims off, takes away); and He cleanses and repeatedly prunes every branch that continues to bear fruit, to make it bear more and richer and more excellent fruit. You are cleansed and pruned already, because of the word which I have given you [the teachings I have discussed with you]. Dwell in Me, and I will dwell in you. [Live in Me, and I will live in you.] Just as no branch can bear fruit of itself without abiding in (being vitally united to) the vine, neither can you bear fruit unless you abide in Me. I am the Vine; you are the branches. Whoever lives in Me and I in him bears much (abundant) fruit. However, apart from Me [cut off from vital union with Me] you can do nothing. If a person does not dwell in Me, he is thrown out like a [broken-off] branch, and withers; such branches are gathered up and thrown into the fire, and they are burned. If you live in Me [abide vitally united to Me] and My words remain in you and continue to live in your hearts, ask whatever you will, and it shall be done for you. When you bear (produce) much fruit, My Father is honored and glorified, and you show and prove yourselves to be true followers of Mine (John 15:1-8 AMP).

In Chapter 3 I said that to abide in Christ means to remain permanently in, continue on in, and be vitally united to Him. It is a work of the Spirit, not the flesh; **it is not a work we perform but a position we rest in**.

Jesus is the Vine, the Father the Gardener. The Father cuts off unfruitful branches but prunes fruitful ones so they will bear even more fruit. The thought of being cut off as an unfruitful branch is quite scary! Acccording to Vine's New Testament Dictionary, the Greek word for "takes away" (cut off) is *airo*, "does not contemplate members of the 'Body' of Christ, but those who (just as a graft which being inserted, does not 'abide' or 'strike') are merely professed followers, giving only the appearance of being joined to the parent stem."[3] If you are truly a child of God by virtue of being born again of the Spirit, then your fears of being "**airoed**" are relieved right now.

Another word for "prune" is **cleanse**, or **purify**. Fruitful branches are purified so they become more fruitful. We are the branches grafted into the Vine to bear the fruit that the Vine produces in us. The life in the Vine flows through us, cleansing and purifying us that we might bear more and greater fruit. Fruit on the branches is the natural result of life in its vine.

What does a branch do? It just hangs there, doesn't it? It doesn't abide in the vine by its own effort, nor does it groan and strain and force itself to produce fruit. It simply abides. It rests in the vine, partaking of the life, strength, and vitality of the vine, and simply bears the fruit that the vine produces.

We are the most beautiful branches you could ever imagine, and there's absolutely nothing we can do on our own to produce the fruit of the Kingdom of God. We are extensions of Jesus, our Vine, and His life flows through us producing fruit. It is His fruit; not yours, not mine, but His. Not only that, but it is His responsibility to produce it in us. Our part is to rest in Him and let Him do it. Apart from Him we can do nothing.

Abiding is our spiritual position in Christ and is a place of rest, not struggle. It means resting in the finished work of Jesus. He did it all for us when He died on the cross. Now He says, "Come to Me, all you who are weary and burdened, and I will give you rest" (Mt. 11:28). Abiding is not our striving to stay close to Him, but our acceptance of our position as branches and our consent to stay on the vine.

Abiding means recognizing a moment-by-moment relationship with Jesus. He is Emmanuel, God with us **now**. We do not walk in the past or the future. We walk in the here and now, and that is where we find Him. He is with us now. Abiding is a "right now" relationship.

Abiding means acknowledging our total dependence on God. It is accepting that our being established in Christ on a day-by-day basis is God's work, not ours. Total dependence is a difficult concept for an independent culture, isn't it? Our inclination is to manage everything for ourselves.

Isaiah 27:3 says that the Lord keeps the vineyard, watering it and protecting it moment by moment, day and night. In the Book of Exodus, God provided manna for the Israelites in the wilderness on a day-by-day basis to teach them to depend on and trust Him. There is an important principle here. God wants our fellowship and awareness of Him to be a moment-by-moment, day-by-day experience.

Abiding means daily committing our lives and spiritual growth to God. Paul exhorts us to offer our bodies as "living sacrifices, holy and pleasing to God...[our] spiritual act of worship" (Rom. 12:1b). This is an offering we must make on a daily, continual basis.

Andrew Murray, in his classic devotional book *Abide in Christ*, sums up this whole idea of abiding beautifully:

"And so each day separately, all the day continually, day by day successively, we abide in Jesus."[4]

How's Your Love Life?

The much-neglected Old Testament book of the Song of Solomon is really a tremendously intimate expression of love. In fact, one pastor I heard of has taught the book as a manual for intimate lovemaking between a husband and a wife. It is a wonderful parable of Christ's love for His Bride, His Church, but I believe it is also an expression of His love to each of us as individuals.

Listen to some of His expressions of love:

Let him kiss me with the kisses of his mouth—for your love is more delightful than wine (Song of Solomon 1:2).

He brought me to the banqueting house, and his banner over me was love [for love waved as a protecting and comforting banner over my head when I was near him] (Song of Solomon 2:4 AMP).

..."Arise, my darling, my beautiful one, and come with me." ...show me your face, let me hear your voice; for your voice is sweet, and your face is lovely (Song of Solomon 2:10,14).

How beautiful you are, my darling! Oh, how beautiful!... All beautiful you are, my darling; there is no flaw in you. ... You have stolen my heart... (Song of Solomon 4:1,7,9).

These are His attitudes toward us. Have you ever imagined that God loved you with this kind of passion, that He longed for this kind of intimate fellowship with you?

The Amplified Bible has a series of questions listed as footnotes to the Song of Solomon that I think are dead on the mark when thinking about our intimacy with God. **How are things between you and Jesus?** As you think about your answer, consider these questions[5]:

- Does my spirit crave the Divine Shepherd, even in the presence of the best that the world can offer me? (Song of Solomon 1:7)

- Do I have a constant sense of my Shepherd's presence, regardless of my surroundings? (Song of Solomon 2:6)

- Do I take time to meet my Good Shepherd each day, letting Him tell me of His love, and cheering His heart with my interest in Him? (Song of Solomon 2:13)

- Do I realize that my voice lifted in praise and song is sweet to Him, or do I withhold it? (Song of Solomon 2:14)

- What is my greatest concern, the thing about which most of all I want Christ's help? When He asks to hear my voice, what do I tell Him? (Song of Solomon 2:15)

- Do I heed Christ when He bids me to come away from the lions' den of temptation and dwell with Him? (Song of Solomon 4:8)

- Am I willing to have the north wind of adversity blow upon me, if it will better fit me for Christ's presence and companionship? (Song of Solomon 4:16)

- In my weariness from earthly cares, do I hesitate to answer when the Divine Shepherd knocks at my door, and so turn Him from me? (Song of Solomon 5:3)

- Is my Savior unquestionably the One altogether lovely, the One above all others most precious to me? Can I tell how and why Christ is more to me than any human being or than all earthly possessions? (Song of Solomon 5:16)

Developing Spiritual Intimacy

It is clear, then, that the Lord loves us with a depth and a passion beyond anything we have ever imagined, and He wants us to share intimate fellowship with Him. How do we walk in that? How can we develop such intimacy with the Lord? Although growth in intimacy is a work of the Spirit and not of the flesh, there are a number of things we can do to condition ourselves for a closer, deeper walk with our Lord.

One way we can grow toward intimacy is to learn what it means to wait upon the Lord. One of the most beautiful promises in all the Old Testament is Isaiah 40:31:

> *But those who wait for the Lord [who expect, look for, and hope in Him] shall change and renew their strength and power; they shall lift their wings and mount up [close to God] as eagles [mount up to the sun]; they shall run and not be weary, they shall walk and not faint or become tired* (AMP).

There are many ideas floating around about what it means to wait on the Lord. Some people feel they should not do anything at all until God moves. Others are simply waiting for Jesus to return. I believe these are wrong concepts of waiting. You can't steer a parked car. Waiting on the Lord is not a passive thing.

While we are sitting around "waiting on the Lord," we may miss the fact that He is ten miles down the road waiting on us! A better concept is the one that views waiting on the Lord as serving Him—waiting upon Him, ready to do His bidding and will—as a waiter serves. This is a solid concept and a great idea, but it still doesn't capture the meaning of the Hebrew word.

"Wait" (*qavah* in Hebrew) means "to bind together by twisting." It also means to expect and to tarry. Those who wait upon the Lord are closely braided together with Him and will exchange their strength for His. Then they will mount up with wings as eagles, run without becoming weary, and walk without fainting. We will exchange our strength for His. Wow! What a promise! As we understand waiting from the perspective of being tightly braided to Him, our intimacy with Christ will grow, and we will see greater fruitfulness in our lives—the fruit of the Spirit and the fruit of ministry.

Another step toward greater intimacy is to place our priorities in the right order. Jesus said in Matthew 6:33, "But seek first His kingdom and His righteousness, and all these things will be given to you as well." This is one time when it's okay to be selfish, to say "me first," because our relationship with Jesus is more important than anything or anyone else. Our first priority should be seeking the things of God's Kingdom and nurturing our prayer and fellowship times with Him.

So often we get things turned around and focus so much attention on daily needs and concerns that we shut Jesus out. Too often I hear people say, "When my husband (or wife) gets saved (or co-operates wtih my agenda), then I'll get my act together with God." "When my children return," or simply, "When I get a good job...." What is more likely to happen is that when these things occur, people will find another problem that will take priority. The promise Jesus gives us is that when we put Him first, He will take care of all the other priorities in our lives. He stands ready to help us. Second Chronicles 16:9a says, "For the eyes of the Lord range throughout the earth to strengthen those whose hearts are fully committed to Him." If only we would understand this, believe it, and take Jesus at His word!

This does not mean abandoning or neglecting the important people or circumstances in our lives. Rather, we trust the Lord to help us bring those relationships into line as we walk in daily intimacy and fellowship with Him. Intimacy and discipleship is not having all the right theological answers, or even having our church membership and all of our doctrines in the right order. It is living in a never-ending love relationship with God. On the one hand it means to quit striving and to trust in and rest in the Lord, and on the other hand to show diligence and desire. They go together, but in the proper order.

Feeding on the Word of God regularly also promotes spiritual intimacy. We need to let the seeds of the Word get thoroughly planted within us. Many of us are spiritual anorexics because we haven't fed on God's Word or let it grow in our lives and produce fruit. It is like being on a starvation diet in the midst of plenty! There is no reason for it. Faith comes by hearing the Word of God (see Rom. 10:17). Faith can also falter through neglecting it. Don't neglect the Word. Read it, study it, meditate on it, and let it move you into deeper love for Jesus.

Finally, spiritual intimacy grows when we pray in the Spirit. This is different from praying spiritual prayers. We pray spiritual prayers in English all the time, I hope. Praying in the spirit means praying in tongues—edifying ourselves, building ourselves up, uttering mysteries and secrets to the Father—and then, with our hearts open wide, hearing Him speak back to us. If you have been baptized in the Spirit and and appropriated the ability to speak, pray, and sing in tongues, please use it. That's what it's for.

There is an expression, "You are what you eat." We become what we pursue.What we expose ourselves to becomes the norm for us. We can train our bodies, our attitudes, and our habits for almost anything we desire. What about training our spirit man to pursue the things of the Spirit of God?

It is going to be a costly decision for any of us to move out into greater intimacy with Jesus, to give up our whole lives to Him. Jesus said:

Take My yoke upon you and learn from Me, for I am gentle and humble in heart, and you will find rest for your souls. For My yoke is easy and My burden is light (Matthew 11:29-30).

I love the concept of being yoked together with Jesus. When oxen are yoked together, one is the lead ox and walks just a little bit ahead of the other one, taking the leadership and the major portion of the weight. Jesus is our lead ox and we need to submit to Him to learn of Him, and to be led and taught by Him.

As we learn to rest in the reality of our freedom in Christ, as we acknowledge and accept our status as His prized possessions, abide in Him, and grow in the intimacy of our walk with Him, then we will be equipped to release the life of the Word into the Body of Christ and into a lost world.

Endnotes

1. Kenneth and Gloria Copeland, *From Faith to Faith: A Daily Guide to Victory* (Fort Worth, TX: KCP Publications, 1992), January 13.

2. James G. Small (1817–1888).

3. W.E. Vine, *An Expository Dictionary of Biblical Words* (Nashville, TN: Thomas Nelson, Inc., 1984).

4. Andrew Murray, *Abide in Christ* (New Candan, CT: Keats Publishing, Inc., 1983).

5. The Amplified Bible, Expanded Edition (Grand Rapids, MI: Zondervan Bible Publishers, 1987), 747-750.

Chapter 6

Releasing the Life of the Word

In the Name of the Lord
We have come to set free
The prisoner, the captive, the slave.

In the Name of the Lord
We now speak liberty
In Jesus, the one who forgave.

Releasers of Life, You have called us to be
Releasers of life, tenderly.
Releasers of life, in your joy laboring,
Releasers of life for the King!

In the Name of the Lord
We deliver from bondage,
In Jesus will be the increase.

In the Name of the Lord
The strong man we engage,
In Jesus will be the release.

We will pierce the darkness
In the Name of the Lord and the King of all kings.[1]

We are called to be releasers of **life** or, to put it another way, releasers of the **Word**. It doesn't matter whether we are men or women, the call is the same. That will come as a great surprise to many women in the Church: "You mean I am called to release the Word of God, right alongside the men?" Absolutely. Look at Psalm 68:11 from the Amplified Bible: "The Lord gives the word [of power]; the women who bear and publish [the news] are a great host." If you check different translations, you will find the words *company* or *army* instead of *women* in many of them. The Hebrew word used here, *tsaba*, is feminine.

It is time to get back to some real basics. We're going to take a fresh look at some Scriptures that relate to the role of women in God's divine order, in the Church, and in ministry leadership in general. There may be many of you who have never viewed these Scriptures in this way before, so get ready to be challenged with a whole new perspective. As we begin to understand from the Word things we have never understood before, we will move in God's grace, mercy, and compassion to begin releasing that river of life within us.

God's Divine Order

God has a divine order in creation that He established from the very beginning. It was in His plan and in place before the first human beings walked on the earth. The fall of man and the corruption of creation due to sin distorted man's understanding of God's divine order. Much of the theology and practice of the Church toward women over the centuries has been based on this distorted view of God's original purpose. However, as Dr. Fuchsia Pickett has stated, "The doctrines of fallen man do not supersede God's divine order."

The Old Testament has much to say regarding the status of women. Almost at the very beginning God made this divine pronouncement:

Then God said, "Let Us make man in Our image, in Our likeness, and let them rule over the fish of the sea and the birds of the air, over the livestock, over all the earth, and over all the creatures that move along the ground." So God created man in His own image, in the image of God He created him; male and female He created them (Genesis 1:26-27).

The Hebrew word translated "man" here is **adam,** a generic term referring to man as a species, humankind as a whole, with no gender distinction. The words used in verse 27 for "male" and "female" are different words entirely and are gender specific. God said, "Let Us make man in Our image…and let **them** rule…." He created **them** male and female. God created male and female and committed to them joint dominion and joint responsibility.

Genesis 2:18 gives a little more detail, "The Lord God said, 'It is not good for the man to be alone. I will make a helper suitable for him.' " It is interesting that this was the one thing in creation that was **not** good. The word **helper** translates a Hebrew word that means to aid or succor, to surround and protect. **Suitable** means a counterpart, one who stands boldly opposite. The New King James Version uses the word **comparable**.

Misunderstandings of these terms and their implications have caused centuries of tyranny, injustice, subjection, and servitude toward women, as well as a concept of female inferiority that has slipped into many areas of the Church. God created woman to be a help and counterpart for man; not secondary to him, but equal in nature, in life, and in commission; having a vital part and responsibility with man in the purposes of God. Physically, mentally, and spiritually, man and woman complement each other.

Matthew Henry, in his commentary written more than 250 years ago, said:

"The woman was made of a rib out of the side of Adam; not made out of his head to rule over him; nor out of his feet to be trampled upon by him; but out of his side to be equal with him, under his arm to be protected, and near his heart to be beloved."[2]

L.E. Maxwell, in his book *Women in Ministry*, says:

"Woman was thus of the same nature as man, of the same flesh and blood, and of the same constitution in all respects. Consequently as woman she had equal powers, faculties, and rights. The very nature of her creation was meant to ensure man's affection and stimulate his esteem. Eve was indeed no mere helpmate. Rather, in her person and constitution, she was suitable to be his companion both socially and intellectually. Eve was not an appendage to Adam but his complement. As Adam's complement, Eve would find her freedom and joy in glad submission to the divine order—a submission as far from servility as heaven is from hell."[3]

Bruce Milne, in his book, *Know the Truth*, sees in Genesis 2:18, "woman's full equality with man. 'A helper fit for him' has the force of 'equal and adequate to.' There is no hint of inferiority; woman is not man's slave or subordinate, but stands in her integrity by his side before God."[4]

Male and female oneness is clearly set forth in the creation account of Genesis. Therefore, any demeaning of a woman, enslaving her, subjecting her, or treating her as inferior or as a second class citizen goes contrary to God's original purpose and plan. Man and woman were created equal in all essential respects: nature, dignity, and commission.[5]

You remember what happened next. Eve was deceived by the serpent and Adam made a deliberate choice to sin. What you may not be aware of is that Eve did not have to hunt for Adam to give him the fruit. He was with her the whole time. Genesis 3:6 says that when Eve saw that the fruit was appealing, "she took some and ate it. She also gave some to her husband, who was with her, and he ate it." Adam was right there with her and did nothing to protect her, or to exercise the authority and dominion he had been given over every living thing, including the serpent.

As a result of their sin, Adam and Eve died spiritually, and the wonderful relationship they had enjoyed with each other and with God was broken. God pronounced a judgment on the serpent: There would be enmity between his offspring and Eve's, and one of her offspring would crush the serpent's head. This was a prophecy concerning Jesus. Even while judging the serpent, God gave a word of blessing and grace to the woman—out of her would come a life that would absolutely destroy the enemy.

Then God said to Eve, "...I will greatly increase your pains in childbearing; with pain you will give birth to children. Your desire will be for your husband, and he will rule over you" (Gen. 3:16). Many religious groups have placed such a strong sensual and sexual connotation to that word **desire**, as if from then on women would be "hot" after their husbands all the time. The Hebrew word (*teshuga*) means "a turning back and forth," "a turning to." The inference here is, "Your turning will be to your husband rather than to

your Lord, and in so doing he will take subjection and dominion and rule over you.''

Ever since that time, men's domination of women has
been treated as a law given and a curse imposed on women.
In reality, it is not a commandment handed down, but a
prophecy, a warning of what the relationship would be between husbands and wives. Male domination with female
subjection is not part of God's divine order in creation, but
a consequence of the fall. Romans 8:2 tells us that Jesus has
set us free from the law of sin and death. That includes everyone, male and female. Because of Jesus Christ, women are
not under some curse spoken to Eve. We are free.

Distortion of God's Divine Order

The Lord promised in Genesis that life to restore mankind's relationship with God would come forth from a
woman. From that day to this the enemy has done everything he could do to cut off that life, to squelch it, to sup-
press in women any expression that has anything to do with
the life of God. There have been centuries of slander, hatred,
and abuse leveled at females that I believe are not cultural or
ethnic, but spiritual and demonic in nature. They are devised
in the heart of the enemy himself, which, by deception, have
kept the concept alive that all women are forever cursed
along with Eve.

Jesus is the fulfillment of the promise to Eve. He is the
great and perfect liberator who came to give us abundant
life (see Jn. 10:10). He set us free from sin and death (see
Rom. 8:2). He became a curse for us to redeem us from the
curse of the law (see Gal. 3:13). He is the Word of God and
His words are life: ''The Spirit gives life; the flesh counts
for nothing. The words I have spoken to you are spirit and
they are life'' (Jn. 6:63). Being the same yesterday, today,

and forever (see Heb. 13:8), He is still the Word of God, and the words He speaks (i.e., anointed words from the mouths of Spirit-filled women and men) are full of Spirit and life.

Everywhere Jesus went, the enemy harassed Him and tried to silence, thwart, or distort the words of life that came from His mouth. First it was opposition from the Pharisees, then betrayal by one of His own, and finally, the cross. Jesus defeated all those attempts when He rose from the dead. **His Word continued on**. During the early days of the Church, the enemy continued his efforts through persecution, harassment, and hardship against Paul, Peter, the other apostles, and the Church as a whole. This has always been one of satan's prime strategies.

In the same way he has tried to thwart life from being released through women. He has tried to stifle **the words of life** that should be coming from us to bring God's wholeness, hope, healing, and restoration. For centuries, satan has done his utmost to muzzle women, not just in religion and ministry, but in everyday life where their words are considered of little value. This is especially true in many Third World nations.

Unfortunately, this mind-set has also strongly influenced the Church. The issue has to do with **speaking**, with releasing the life and the spoken word. Jesus said that out of the overflow of the heart the mouth speaks (see Mt. 12:34), and there is an attempt of the enemy to keep vital words of life from coming forth out of women. In many Christian circles, women can do many jobs, just not ones that involve speaking or teaching. A man may preach the Word, but a woman can only bring a blessing. Although a "blessing" can be spoken, it cannot be considered "preaching." Isn't that ridiculous! A woman may speak during the week at any particular service, but not in the Sunday services. What's the difference?

In the Old Testament, there was tremendous liberty for women who were prophets (i.e., spokesmen). The prophetic ministry was considered the highest form of teaching. Many women took prophetic leadership: Miriam, Huldah, Isaiah's wife, and many others, including Deborah. Deborah was not only a prophet, but also a prime minister during the period of the judges. I understand that, lately, there is a large body of evidence being gathered that may indicate women had priestly duties in the tabernacle worship.

Something came along to reverse this. The oral tradition, or *Talmud*, grew up alongside the Mosaic Law as a commentary and supplement to it. Some of the *Talmud* expressed extreme disdain, subjection, and ugly degradation of women. By New Testament times, the *Talmud* was considered equal in authority to the *Torah*, the Law. In addition, many aspects of Judaism had become Hellenized, or greatly influenced by Greek philosophy and culture. Aristotle, for example, put a badge of inferiority and servility upon women. Such pagan philosophy influenced the Christian Church as Hellenistic ideas were mingled with Christian theology, producing a whole host of beliefs that were pagan at their source and that, unfortunately, still influence aspects of the Church today.

In the early Christian Church there was tremendous liberty where women, along with men, preached the good news of the Kingdom. They realized that they were equal in Christ—called, filled, and anointed by Him equally. In her book *Beyond the Curse*, Aida Spencer writes:

> "The New Testament records many women leaders, women of significant authoritative positions, to mention only a few: Junia is called an apostle; Anna is called a prophet; Philip's four daughters prophesied

as did the women at Corinth; Priscilla and the women at Crete were teachers: The women at Crete were elders, Priscilla was as well a co-worker and a church overseer. The Elect Lady and the Elect Sister were church overseers. Phoebe was a church overseer and a minister. Stephana, possibly a woman, was clearly a person in authority, and a co-worker. Lydia and Chloe were church overseers, and perhaps as well were the mother of Mark, Nympha, and Apphia, Euodia [What names! Where is Mary, Sally, Helen?], Syntyche, Tryphaena, Tryphosa, and possibly, Mary, and Persis were Paul's colleagues, each having their own positions of authority. Even the Jezebel of Revelation 2 was recognized as a teacher, the problem was in what she taught.

"Why have Bible scholars not highlighted these women for us? Have some translators and commentators refused to allow, or never even consider the possibility that women could be in a place of leadership? The reasoning goes something like this: Phoebe could not be a minister, because she was a woman. Junia could not be a woman, because she was an apostle. The Elect Lady must be a church, because she could not be a lady. Stephana could not be a woman, because people were subjected to her.

"Possibly the lack of recognizing the extent of women's ministries in the scriptures, is that we, as women, have not taken the opportunity to study the Bible in an in depth manner, and see that as our Biblical sisters were called, God still calls women to minister His Word of Life today."[6]

Three passages from Paul's Epistles are the primary sources of the Church teachings that have suppressed and silenced women through the centuries: First Corinthians 14:34-35, First Timothy 2:11-14, and Ephesians 5:21-32. Paul is not the villain, though. Poor Paul has been slandered for generations. Much recent biblical scholarship has brought to light the ways Paul has been misunderstood and misinterpreted in these verses. Since the second and third centuries these Scriptures, especially the Corinthian and Timothy portions, have been used to put women into bondage, fear, and condemnation. That is not the action of a loving heavenly Father. Notice that I said the second and third centuries, not the early Church.

The scope of this book will allow only the discussion of the first two of these Scriptures. The Corinthian portion has to do with a worship service; the Timothy portion, with study. Concerning the third Scripture, Ephesians 5:21-32, it will have to suffice to say that Paul's discussion of husbands and wives, and submission, marital love, and respect is given in connection with Christ's love for His Bride, His Church. Submission in marriage is a mutual act between husband and wife. If the wife is to be in submission to her husband, the husband is to regard his wife as someone he would lay down his life for as Christ did for the Church. That is hardly the attitude one would take toward a suppressed, subjected, and subservient person.

The Pauline Teaching: 1 Corinthians 14:34-35

Women should remain silent in the churches. They are not allowed to speak, but must be in submission, as the Law says. If they want to inquire about something, they should ask their own husbands at home;

for it is disgraceful for a woman to speak in the church (1 Corinthians 14:34-35).

Proper Bible study should always follows what's called the historical, grammatical, and critical method, or "HGC." Consider the historical setting, the grammatical structure, and the critical evaluation of the portion of Scripture you are studying in light of all the rest of Scripture. Otherwise, you can make any passage of Scripture mean anything you want it to mean.

This passage in First Corinthians is in the context of orderliness in public worship. Paul has just given instructions for the orderly expression in worship of hymns, words of knowledge, words of prophecy, and tongues, and concludes with his statement about women being silent in church. The very presence of women in worship with the men went against both Jewish and pagan practice. In the synagogues, women were separated from the men, relegated to a side room or balcony as silent observers only. Pagan practice excluded them from worship entirely.

Paul's encouragement of Christian men and women worshiping, praying, and prophesying together was a shockingly radical concept for his pagan and Jewish contemporaries. First century Jewish women participated very little in public life because of the fear of being viewed as promiscuous. Considered inferior to men and very limited in their capabilities, they were not expected to be educated. The condition of Greek wives was even worse. They were kept secluded, their only function to produce legitimate offspring. They took no part in public affairs and never appeared at meals or social occasions.

Public women in this culture—the educated and the well-dressed, adorned with cosmetics and jewelry—were the courtesans, the upper-class prostitutes. In Corinth, most of these women were priestesses at the temple of Aphrodite, the Greek goddess of love. Sexual intercourse was a part of their religious ritual.

With women coming into the Church from these restrictive, isolated backgrounds, it is easy to imagine the scene when they became Christians, set free by Jesus. All of a sudden they were one in Him with men, able to participate in public worship and interact freely with other men and women. It was a whole new world for them. When they came together there was a lot of noise and disorder, especially on the part of the women, because they were not accustomed to listening to public speakers or to participating in public worship.

G.H. Lang gives insight regarding the background and setting of this controversial passage:

> "The persons who mostly formed the churches as at Corinth, were not educated, disciplined westerners, to whom routine and decorum (not to say deadness), especially in public worship, have become second nature and seem wholly proper. On the contrary, they were...nervous, restless, emotional...impulsive, vivacious, talkative; to whom routine was irksome and dullness intolerable...Nor had those first believers been trained to a deadly propriety in public services. Their heathen temples had little semblance of order or sense of stillness."[7]

The Corinthians were boastful, arrogant, and quarrelsome, and had begun to use their knowledge and rights as license, speaking in tongues and prophesying in a disorderly manner. The women were boisterous, flaunting their freedom in

Christ. To such women Paul said, "Hush, be quiet." He was not commanding them not to prophesy, but instructing them how to behave when others were speaking.

Aida Spencer reminds us that, actually, three groups of people were "silenced" or "brought into submission" in chapter 14: speakers in tongues when there was no interpreter (14:27-28), one prophet when a revelation was made to another prophet (14:30-31), and women learning in a shameful manner (14:33-35), because God is a God of peace and not of disorder.[8]

The Greek word for "silent" here means to be quiet, to hush, and to give attention to the speaker. The type of talking that the women were doing is described by the same Greek word that means gossip, prattle, or inattentive talking and babble. These women had never been taught to listen; they were uneducated and disruptive, and Paul is simply dealing here with excesses. It appears that self-control is the issue, rather than silence as we think of it. He would say the same thing today if it were necessary—to men as well as to women.

The obvious thing is that these verses have nothing to do with prohibiting women from preaching, prophesying, praying, or taking leadership in the church. That's not what Paul is talking about. In fact, earlier in the same letter he clearly implies that women did pray and prophesy in the church (see 1 Cor. 11:5).

As far as being "in submission, as the Law says," the Greek word for "submission" here means "a voluntary attitude of being responsive to the needs of others." What "Law" Paul refers to here is debatable. There is no such command for women in the Old Testament. Some scholars think Paul has in mind local civil laws designed to curb religious and cultic excesses of women. Others believe he refers to the Talmud, the Jewish oral tradition, and others believe he could be referring to *agape*, the law of love. Regarding the latter, Paul says in Romans 13:10 that love is the fulfillment of the law. At any rate, it was important to the early Church that the behavior of their women should be above reproach, in sharp contrast to the pagan temple prostitutes, and within the bounds of the law.

It should be noted here that these verses in First Corinthians 14 refer primarily to married women; hence the reference to them asking their husbands at home. These people lived in a culture where home life and marital relations between husband and wife were quite barren. Typically, there was little interaction between them. One writer suggests that Paul wanted to encourage loving communication between spouses, especially when the wives were eager to learn about Jesus.

Eugene H. Peterson, in his marvelous contemporary language translation of the New Testament, *The Message*, captures the true flavor of these verses remarkably well:

Wives must not disrupt worship, talking when they should be listening, asking questions that could more appropriately be asked of their husbands at home. Wives have no license to use the time of worship for unwarranted speaking (1 Corinthians 14:34-35).

The Pauline Teaching: 1 Timothy 2:11-14

A woman should learn in quietness and full submission. I do not permit a woman to teach or to have authority over a man; she must be silent. For Adam was formed first, then Eve. And Adam was not the one deceived; it was the woman who was deceived and became a sinner (1 Timothy 2:11-14).

Did you know that the Church has built an entire doctrine and practice of refusing women verbal ministry and leadership based on this one text? No other aspect of church life has been formed on such a narrow basis. Most theologians agree that a principle has to be found in at least three places. Also remember the HGC method of study. There is now a large body of evidence strongly suggesting that this text has been misunderstood from the original Greek, and therefore mistranslated.

The culprit is the Greek word ***authentein***, translated in the King James Version as "usurp authority," and found **nowhere else** in the Scriptures and only rarely in other Greek literature. Part of the problem is that this word, like so many words in virtually every language, has changed meaning through the centuries. In classic Greek, 400 years before Jesus, *authentein* meant to initiate, to be responsible for a murder, with also some inference to suicide. Around the second or third century after Christ, it began to mean to rule, or to have authority over. By A.D. 600 it meant to have ownership of property, either rightfully, or wrongfully through fraud. At the same time it came to mean usurping of authority, or being domineering. In the day when Paul was writing, *authentein* was a rare verb with a very vulgar connotation, meaning to involve someone in soliciting sexual liaisons. *Authentein* also meant to be the author of or claim to be the originator of something.

Why would Paul use such a vulgar, uncommon term when writing to Timothy about the Ephesian church? An understanding of this will also shed light on Paul's puzzling reference to Adam and Eve in verses 13 and 14.

Timothy was a young man who served as overseer for the church in Ephesus. The believers in the church had been converted from a pagan background steeped in the occult and loaded with myths and genealogies, doctrines of demons, and every weird thing under the sun. Ephesus was a center for the worship of the Greek goddess Diana, which involved such teachings as female superiority and domination over men, female procreation without male involvement, and all kinds of sexual perversions and fertility rites. On top of everything else, the heretical Gnostic cult began to infiltrate the Church. This quasi-Christian group made a complete distinction between the spiritual (which was pure) and the material (which was evil). This led to immorality because they claimed that nothing the body did could "tarnish" the purity of the spirit. They actually denied Christ's humanity, declaring that He, being spirit, could not have died.

It is easy to see the challenge Paul and young Timothy faced—new, ignorant converts mingling their old, pagan, demonic doctrines with Gnosticism and Old Testament teaching. Someone has said that Gnosticism was the first century equivalent of the New Age movement. Now we can understand some of what Paul's instructions were to Timothy: "As I urged you when I went into Macedonia, stay there in Ephesus so that you may command certain men not to teach false doctrines any longer nor to devote themselves to myths and endless genealogies..." (1 Tim. 1:3-4). Also, "Oppose false teaching." "Warn people about doctrines of demons." "Stop stupid, senseless controversies." "Use the Scriptures—rightly divide the Word—train yourself to be godly."

Gnostics taught that there were levels of secret, higher, superior knowledge revealed only to those who were specially initiated—mediators between God and man. Many of these supposed mediators were women, promising godliness if their hearers would follow their "teaching." Now you can see why Paul emphasized to Timothy in First Timothy 2:5, "For there is one God and one mediator between God and men, the man Christ Jesus." These women were deluded, deceived, and untaught. No wonder Paul says, "Let your women learn" (see 1 Tim. 2:11)!

That confusing verse about Adam being formed before Eve seems out of place in the context of teachings about prayer and learning. Now it is going to make more sense as we see the heretical teaching that Paul was addressing as it was filtering into the Church. One major Gnostic teaching declared that the creator was the serpent—the revealer of truth, the illuminator. Eve was exalted as the one who brought life to Adam. She ate of the tree of the knowledge of good and evil; she received special knowledge from God, which had been hidden from them, and taught this new revelation to Adam. Rather than calling this act sin, the Gnostics regarded it as a sign of superiority. They taught that Eve was the mother, the forerunner of all (*authentein*, originator), that she came first and that Adam was born from her. Not so, said Paul. He was simply bringing correction to erroneous, cultic teaching that had come into the Church.

Catherine Kroegar, Hebrew and Greek researcher, puts forth the theory that since *authentein* had a sexual connotation as well, Paul was exhorting the women not to involve a man in the heretical kind of Christianity that taught licentious behavior as one of its doctrines. Such a female did indeed "teach to fornicate" in the Thyatiran church, mentioned in Revelation 2:20 (KJV).[9]

Paul's instructions concerning women in First Timothy 2 come at the end of guidelines regarding worship, and particularly prayer. In verse 8 he exhorts the men to pray "without anger or disputing" among themselves. The women's behavior was to be in like manner. Also, they were to dress modestly, in sharp contrast to the pagan women around them. Paul wanted the women to be taught, a concept that was unthinkable and radical, yet here he is writing, "a woman should learn"—a principle that came in with the Christian Church. Women were not accustomed to listening to teachers or spending time in study. His instructions were for them to do so in silence, with all subjection, or submission. The word for "subjection" here is the same one found in the Corinthian passage as well as in Ephesians 5. It means the voluntary willingness to be responsive to the needs of another; in this case, their own needs to listen and hear, and the needs of the teachers to communicate without noisy competition. The word for "silence" here does not mean refraining from talking. It means harmony, peace, conformity, agreement, and restful quietness, in meditation or study. It was an attitude of the heart while learning. It has nothing to do with speaking.

In First Corinthians 14:34, the word *sigao* means to be quiet while someone else is speaking; in First Timothy 2:11, *hesuchia* means to be quiet within oneself, in order to listen attentively. This attitude of silence was one that students gave to rabbinical instruction; it was a posture for learning.

That confusing verse about Adam being formed before Eve seems out of place in the context of teachings about prayer and learning. Perhaps some of the mystery has been cleared up; unorthodox teaching was a prominent problem in the Ephesian church. Obviously, orthodox teaching was needed for correction. The women were being deceived—not only being led away by false doctrines, but probably propagating these teachings as well. No wonder Paul commanded them to learn while not allowing them to teach, especially with the particular "Diana/Gnostic" methods of teaching men. He was dealing with a current crisis within the Church.

According to the Greek grammatical structure and verb tenses, Paul is saying, "I am not presently allowing a woman to teach." In fact, the strong command here is "let her learn" (and while she is learning she is not allowed to teach). Another researcher adds this: "I am not permitting a woman to teach *authentein*" (to proclaim woman to be the originator of man). Remember the phrase "usurp authority" was not used in this era. This is precisely the reason Paul prohibited them from teaching; not because they were women, but because they were ignorant of the truth. They were still too young in the Christian faith and too close to their pagan past to teach Christian truth with knowledge and authority.

It should be clear by now that these Scriptures have absolutely nothing to do with Christian women being prohibited from the verbal ministry of releasing the spoken word. No matter what social, ethnic, or structural expression of the Body of Christ they come from, the daughters of God are chosen, called, anointed, and appointed by Him to do the works of the Kingdom, including releasing His life and releasing the spoken, audible Word.

Endnotes

1. Jeremy Sinnott, "Releasers of Life," © 1997, Rejoice Publishing and Productions. Used by permission.

2. Matthew Henry, *Commentary on the Whole Bible*, New One Volume Edition, Rev. Leslie F. Church, ed. (Grand Rapids, MI: Zondervan Publishing House, 1961), 7.

3. L.E. Maxwell, *Women in Ministry* (Wheaton, IL: Victor Books, Scripture Press Publications, Inc., 1987), 33.

4. Bruce Milne, *Know The Truth* (Downers Grove, IL: Inter-Varsity Press, 1982), 99.

5. Maxwell, *Women in Ministry.*

6. Aida Spencer, *Beyond the Curse: Women Called to Ministry*, (Peabody, MA: Hendrickson Publishers, Inc., 1985), 120.

7. G.H. Lang, *The Churches of God* (London: C.J. Thynne & Jarvis, 1928), as noted in L.E. Maxwell, *Women in Ministry*, 87.

8. Spencer, *Beyond the Curse*, 104.

9. Catherine C. Kroegar, "Ancient Heresies and a Strange Greek Verb," *The Reformed Journal*, 29 (March 1979), 14.

Chapter 7

No Turning Back

When we were preparing for our daughter's marriage several years ago, I decided it was time to clean the house and perk things up a bit. I bought some super new wallpaper for the front hall along with some companion wallpaper for the little downstairs bathroom that is visible from the hallway. At that time I got the front hall wallpaper on, but did not do the bathroom. For four years the turquoise Chinese wallpaper in the bathroom clashed with the new wallpaper in the hall.

One day I was looking at that bathroom wallpaper and, curious as to how well it was attached, pulled at a corner of it. A small piece came off in my hand. Fortunately, it was on the side you can't see from the hall, because I didn't have the time then to put up the new paper.

Finally, about a year later, I walked in the house one Sunday night after I had been teaching. I was very tired. When I went into that bathroom, I looked at where I had ripped off the paper and wondered how long it would take to clear off the rest of it. Reaching over, I grabbed a strip at the bottom and all of a sudden the entire piece was in my hand. Out of my mouth came the words, "No turning back." The next day I began tearing all the paper off. My patience was taxed to the limit as I struggled to remove the old paper (who said "dry-strippable" came right off?) and get the new on. It had stuff like crazy glue on the back. It was stuck and I couldn't move it. I didn't finish until after 2 o'clock in the morning, by which time I was frustrated and irritable. There was no turning back, though. Once I put my hand to the task, I had to carry on.

New in Christ

When a person is born again by the Spirit of God, he has made a new beginning and there really is no turning back. Remember Second Corinthians 5:17, which says that anyone who is in Christ is completely new; the old is gone. Jesus made reference to this irreversible quality of the new life in Him:

Neither do men pour new wine into old wineskins. If they do, the skins will burst, the wine will run out and the wineskins will be ruined. No, they pour new wine into new wineskins, and both are preserved (Matthew 9:17).

Jesus was talking about the futility and danger of trying to mingle the old with the new—old traditions with new revelation or old ideas with new understanding. The old is too inflexible to contain the new and both will be ruined by trying. None of us who are born again are old wineskins. We are new wineskins filled with new life from the Spirit. He does not simply dress up the old to make do, but creates something totally new.

The writer of Hebrews expresses the same idea of moving forward with no turning back:

Therefore, since we are surrounded by such a great cloud of witnesses, let us throw off everything that hinders and the sin that so easily entangles, and let us run with perseverance the race marked out for us. Let us fix our eyes on Jesus, the author and perfecter of our faith, who for the joy set before Him endured the cross, scorning its shame, and sat down at the right hand of the throne of God (Hebrews 12:1-2).

In the race of life that is before us, we must throw off everything that hinders us—empty traditions, past sins, and past regrets—and move steadily forward with our eyes firmly fixed on Jesus. What in your past would distract you from moving forward in Christ? You cannot redeem the past. You can neither change the past nor return to it. Yet satan tries to keep you in bondage to your memories.

Jesus Christ is Emmanuel, God with us **now**. We experienced the miracle of the new birth and were placed in Christ. Our healing, deliverance, and victory would proceed much faster if we would simply acknowledge who we are in Him. As He heals our memories and renews our minds, we will walk in the freedom that is ours. If we choose to turn back and cry over the past, then we will never experience the wholeness or rest that He has for us.

When a prophetic word came that a fresh wind of the Spirit was blowing and filling our sails to move on, I envisioned the Church as a great and glorious sailing craft with billowing sails on a lake, with the wind of God blowing His Spirit into us. He has given us a new day, a new hope, and a new beginning with Him. Jesus is pouring the new wine into us. He is oiling us with His Spirit, making us pliable and soft in His hands as He soaks us with the water of His Word, getting rid of all our wrinkles and hindrances to walking in

Him. He is molding us into something fresh and new and good. He wants us to move on with Him.

The Danger of Turning Back

Throughout the Scriptures there are people who persisted in looking back, turning back, or desiring to. They wanted to cling to the past, to their old lives and their old ways of doing things; they wanted to hold fast to the familiar and the comfortable. They were afraid or unwilling to move forward to fulfill the potential God had given them and the plan He had for them. Turning back to the past incapacitated them for walking in the present. Quite often their backward-looking attitudes were accompanied by **profane words** against God. Merriam-Webster's dictionary defines "profane" as "to treat something sacred with abuse, irreverence, or contempt."[1] Refusing to take God at His word and move out in faith as He leads is a form of profanity because it holds God in contempt.

In Luke 17:32 Jesus said, "Remember Lot's wife!" He made this statement in the midst of a discussion regarding the day of the Lord and the judgment. When that day appeared, it would come so swiftly that no one would have time to return home to grab anything. It would come as swiftly as destruction had come on Sodom and Gomorrah.

The incident Jesus referred to is recorded in Genesis 19. Lot, Abraham's nephew, along with Lot's wife and daughters, had to flee the city of Sodom before the Lord destroyed it. God warned them not to delay or look back. Lot's wife disobeyed, looked back upon the doomed city, and became a pillar of salt. In an instant she was totally incapacitated for any future life or usefulness. She may have succumbed to curiosity, or she may have regretted the loss of her material world, her belongings, and her old relationships. Nevertheless, judgment engulfed her because her affections were with Sodom rather than with God. Jesus warned us to remember her example. Turning back is dangerous. It can even be deadly.

When the Israelites reached the Red Sea they began grumbling against Moses and against God. How quickly they had forgotten their miraculous deliverance from Egyptian slavery! Now they faced the unknown. They were afraid to move ahead. They were afraid of the wilderness. Their minds turned back to what they had left behind in Egypt, and that seemed more appealing than their present circumstances. They profaned God by desiring to return to slavery rather than to walk in the freedom He had given them. Nevertheless, God delivered them again at the Red Sea, destroying the pursuing Egyptian army and leading the Israelites across the sea on dry land. Such a great display of the power and glory of God filled the Israelites with awe and they feared and worshiped Him.

Their newfound reverence for the Lord lasted exactly three days, until they reached a place called Marah. They were thirsty and the only water available there was bitter and undrinkable. Perhaps if they had drunk it anyway, God would have carried out a thorough cleansing, like a giant "dose of salts," purging from their systems any vestiges of their past in Egypt. Instead, the people groaned and murmured against Moses and God. Again God delivered. At God's command, Moses threw a particular tree limb into the water, making it drinkable.

This pattern was repeated time after time. God provided and the people worshiped, for a time. Then they were right back in their old routine of doubting God and challenging

Moses. The last straw came when the 12 spies sent to scout out the land returned to report to Moses and the people (see Num. 13–14). Ten of the spies gave a very negative report. Despite the bounty of the land, they said, the inhabitants were too strong for the Israelites to overcome. Of the 12 spies, only Joshua and Caleb were willing to trust and follow the Lord. When the people listened to the ten spies and rejected God, He condemned them to wander in the wilderness for 40 years until all of that rebellious generation died. Of all the people over the age of 20, only Joshua and Caleb would live to enter the land.

God's patience was at an end. In Numbers 14:22, God says that the Israelites had murmured against Him and tested Him ten times. They had profaned His name, holding Him in contempt. As a result of their rebellion, unbelief, and profanity, what should have been a short journey for the Israelites became a 40-year marathon. God continued to provide for them: manna, water, quail, and shoes and clothes that did not wear out, but the people continued to complain. Once their minds and hearts were set on the past, they had no vision, no hope for the future. They would not believe that God could lead them into victory and freedom.

The Importance of Moving Forward

Looking back can have the same effect on us as Christians. Christ has delivered us, and He wants to lead us into victory, freedom, and fruitful abundance. Many of us, however, out of ignorance, fear, or rebellion, choose to remain in the desert land of "what if" and "if only." We can't let go of the past or trust that God's way will lead us into a brighter and better future. We need to stop looking behind, focus our minds and our faith squarely on the Lord, and move out boldly into the purpose and plan He has for us.

When we focus on the Lord, incredible untapped rivers of potential and opportunity come into view:

Do not [earnestly] remember the former things; neither consider the things of old. Behold, I am doing a new thing! Now it springs forth; do you not perceive and know it and will you not give heed to it? I will even make a way in the wilderness and rivers in the desert (Isaiah 43:18-19 AMP).

If we dwell on the past we will miss out on God's work in the present. If we focus on the old, we will not see the new thing He is doing. "Behold" means "pay attention." God wants us to pay attention to the new thing He is doing. Let the past be the past. Forget the hurts, the sorrows, the regrets, and the disappointments of the past. Let go of the anger and the guilt and the sense of failure. Don't dwell on those things. They are in the dry, stony desert. Let God do a new thing in your life, to make a way in the wilderness of confusion and to turn the desert into fertile, well-watered soil.

Moving forward means giving our undivided attention to serving Christ. Jesus said in Luke 9:62 that "No one who puts his hand to the plow and looks back is fit for service in the kingdom of God." This has nothing to do with backsliding or losing one's salvation. Jesus is saying that serving Him requires our full attention and concentration. Half-hearted discipleship hinders us from maximum usefulness in God's Kingdom. We need to let Jesus be the Savior of our past as well as of our present and future. If we focus on our Sodom or our Egypt, we cannot be wholehearted for Him. When we put our hands to the plow we need to focus our eyes on Jesus.

What vision or purpose or goal has the Holy Spirit placed before you? What ministry has He called you to? If you are not sure, ask Him to reveal it to you. He wants you to know. He wants you to see Him. You need to see God's vision.

Noah had a vision of the ark. God described it to him and told him how to build it. That vision sustained Noah for over a century as he followed God's instructions and built a huge wooden boat miles and miles from any water, even though he was likely subjected to much persecution and mocking. That's vision.

Abraham had a vision of being the father of many nations and a blessing to the world, even though he had no children and was beyond child-bearing age—as good as dead, the Bible says (see Rom. 4:19). He had faith that God would do what He had promised though, and Isaac was born when Abraham was 100 years old. Abraham had lived for and expected this vision for 25 years.

Paul had a vision of sharing the gospel with the Gentile world. This vision sustained him through beatings, stonings, shipwrecks, harassment, persecution, slander, and innumerable other hardships. If anyone could have been hampered by his past, it was Paul. He did not let that happen, though. He let it all go and pressed ahead because of his vision:

Brothers, I do not consider myself yet to have taken hold of it. But one thing I do: Forgetting what is behind and straining toward what is ahead, I press on toward the goal to win the prize for which God has called me heavenward in Christ Jesus (Philippians 3:13-14).

Paul understood the power of vision and the peril of the past.

Jesus had a vision of redeeming mankind and reconciling us to God. That vision sustained Him as He endured the pain and humiliation of the cross and the weight of the sins of the world on His shoulders. He looked ahead to the joy set before Him, as Hebrews 12:2 says.

Vision is for the future, not the past. Our usefulness in the Kingdom of God is proportional to the scope of our vision. We won't get anywhere by constantly looking behind us. We must look ahead to Jesus and move forward with confidence.

Hindrances to Moving Forward

One of the keys to releasing the principles of God in our life is the way we use our tongue. Kelley Varner, in *The More Excellent Ministry*, wrote, "The secret to life and health is a mouth filled with words of life. Our lips and our speech must be in agreement with His Word and Spirit."[2] The children of Israel profaned God for years, holding Him in contempt with their murmuring lips and rebellious hearts. This is blasphemy, or slander against God. We do the same thing whenever we doubt God, disobey Him, or speak ill of ourselves with regard to what He says He has done in us and for us.[3]

Do two walk together unless they have agreed to do so? (Amos 3:3)

The tongue has the power of life and death, and those who love it will eat its fruit (Proverbs 18:21).

The tongue that brings healing is a tree of life, but a deceitful tongue crushes the spirit (Proverbs 15:4).

Truthful lips endure forever, but a lying tongue lasts only a moment (Proverbs 12:19).

The mouth of the righteous is a fountain of life, but violence overwhelms the mouth of the wicked (Proverbs 10:11).

We can sow life to ourselves and to others or we can sow profanity. "Profanity is any speech that comes out of our mouth that is not in agreement with the letter and the Spirit of the Word of God...words that are not in agreement with the Christ nature."[4] We need to learn the language of the Kingdom of God. As children we had to learn to walk and talk in the natural world. Now, as our hearts are being changed, we must learn to walk and talk in the Kingdom. This means learning to speak words of faith and hope, not of condemnation and fear.

Our words reveal to others where we are in God. Our speech identifies us, and it can betray us. We often profane God by thoughtlessly defiling Him, His salvation, His infilling, and even His very presence. Remember, He is in us and has given us His name to use with authority.

Kelley Varner lists a number of common profanities among Christians. Each one is an excuse for not moving on into the future. Following are some examples[5]:

"I'm only human, you know." A variation of that is, "It's just my nature. It's just my nature to be fearful, or unforgiving, or to have temper tantrums. That's the way I am." No, that's turning back. Those are traits of the old nature. Christ has given us a new nature. If we walk in that new nature, we can overcome the qualities of the old one.

"I'm going to." One pastor called this "serving the god of gonna." "I'm gonna do better. I'm gonna get my life together. I'm gonna get all my healing and my deliverance." This is the lifestyle of good intentions. It's what we are going to do someday, but never seem to get around to. Well, today is the day of salvation. Jesus is Emmanuel, God with us **now**. He is here **now**. He is speaking **now**. He wants us to do His will **now**. He wants us to flow with Him now, not live in the past or wait for some future time. He wants us to move with Him **now**. He is the Almighty God who enables and indwells right **now** anyone who is cooperative and submissive to Him.

"I can't." In all honesty, this one is more a matter of willingness than ability. "I can't (won't) minister to anyone. I can't (won't) keep my eyes on Jesus. I can't (won't) share the Word." How can you know if you never try? Philippians 4:13 says we can do everything through Him who gives us strength. Without Him we can do nothing. With Him all things are possible. Perhaps "I can't" reflects past failures in things that weren't initiated by God in the first place, or ignorance as to how to take dominion over thoughts and attitudes that rise up against the true knowledge of Christ.

"What if." This one will paralyze you right on the spot. "What if it is not of God? What if it doesn't work? What if they don't receive me? What if I fail? What if I make a mistake?" This particular profanity is sparked by the spirit of fear. It is not of God. Faith is a spiritual force that comes by hearing and meditating on the Word of God. Fear is a spiritual force too, one that comes by meditating on the word of the devil. All of us have jumped ahead of God at times, but He gently restores and corrects us. He is the God of the second, third, fourth, and umpteenth chance. People who use this curse word know that the hardest thing to do is to begin. If we are constantly paralyzed by the past and are afraid of the future, we will never step out and put our necks on the line.

"We've always done it this way before," or its variation, "We've never done it this way before." This one is sometimes called the "seven last words of the church." Either way, does that make it right? If we are not willing to stretch and change, we're going to have a tough time, because things change when people begin moving with the Lord. Many of the things we have "always done" come from the traditions of men or from an old order of legalism that has the form of godliness but denies its power (see 2 Tim. 3:5). People in that situation are in bondage. The Lord may want us to try some new things, things we've never done before, to break us out of the mold of sameness. We need to discern what the Spirit is doing today and move with Him.

"I'm afraid of what people will think about me." We wouldn't be bothered so much by what other people think of us if we realized how rarely they do. What does it matter what other people say or think? Whether it is criticism or praise, we should get to the place where it doesn't move us one way or the other. We might as well accept the fact right now that we won't please all the people all the time. Some people become such man-pleasers that they literally become slaves to others. Proverbs 29:25 says the fear of man is a snare. The majority is not always right. Somebody has to stand up and be counted. Will it be you? Will it be me? God is love and there is no fear in Him. First John 4:18 says that "perfect love drives out fear, because fear has to do with punishment." The one who fears is not yet mature in love.

"But..." Very simply, this is one of the deadliest and most paralyzing curse words of unbelief. More potential is unrealized and more lives experience defeat because of this one profanity than probably any other. There is no "but..." with God.

"Maybe." This is a word of uncertainty, indecision, and double-mindedness. It feeds doubt in our minds and prevents us from acting. Since we can't decide what to do, we do nothing.

Whatever our reason for not moving in God, there is a strong verse somewhere in the Bible that will help us to renew our minds and go on to the maturity, fruitfulness, hope, joy, and everything else that our salvation holds for us.

The psalmist sums up all of this beautifully:

May the words of my mouth and the meditation of my heart be pleasing in Your sight, O Lord, my Rock and my Redeemer (Psalm 19:14).

Endnotes

1. *Merriam-Webster's Collegiate Dictionary*, 10th Edition (Springfield, MA: Merriam-Webster, Inc., 1994), 930.

2. Kelley Varner, *The More Excellent Ministry* (Shippensburg, PA: Destiny Image Publishers, Inc., 1988), 177.

3. Varner, *The More Excellent*, 185.

4. Varner, *The More Excellent*, 178.

5. Varner, *The More Excellent*, 194-199.

Chapter 8

Five Needed Negatives

As we move forward in our freedom in Christ, determined not to turn back but to press on toward the goal of becoming releasers of life, there are many things we need to consider. All of us, I am sure, understand the importance of being positive in our attitudes, words, and actions. We should be careful never to let anything negative escape from our lips, right? Nevertheless, I think there are five negatives, five biblical negatives, that we need to consider. They are really positives in disguise, and will help us in our growth and understanding as we walk in faith with the Lord and move into the ministry of releasing life into the Body of Christ. These are five needed negatives.

Fear Not

What is the one thing that you fear the most? Are you afraid of what someone else thinks about you? Do you fear someone in your family? Are you afraid that you will have no meat for tomorrow's dinner? Do you fear getting sick? Most of our fears we would never confess openly. Instead, when they come, they just nibble away inside us.

Did you know that the Bible contains 366 "fear nots" or the equivalent? That is one for every day of the year plus one more for leap year. They begin in Genesis and run right through to Revelation. Any subject that turns up that frequently in the Bible must be near to God's heart. He does not want His children to live in fear.

The first biblical "fear not" is in Genesis 15:1: "After this, the word of the Lord came to Abram in a vision: 'Do not be afraid, Abram. I am your shield, your very great reward.' " It seems that every time a person in the Bible received a special visitation from God or an angel, the first thing that was said to the person was "fear not." Fear is the natural human response to being in the presence of the Divine. So, the Lord said to Abram, "Fear not." He then promised Abram that a son from his own body would inherit his estate, and through that son Abram would become the father of a countless multitude. Genesis 15:6 says that Abram believed God, and that was credited to him as righteousness. First came the word of comfort, "fear not"; then the promise; then the belief in Abram's heart.

The last "fear not" in the Bible is in Revelation 1:17: "When I saw Him, I fell at His feet as though dead. Then He placed His right hand on me and said: 'Do not be afraid. I am the First and the Last.' " John's first reaction on seeing the Lord was to fall at His feet out of fear and the power of the Lord's presence. Again, the Lord's first words were of comfort: "Fear not." He comforted John further by identifying Himself as the Lord, the Living One who controlled history and life and death. John needed to be reassured and released from fear before he could handle the great revelations concerning the endtimes that were about to be made known to him.

Fear comes with separation from God. When Adam and Eve disobeyed God, the fellowship they had always enjoyed with Him was broken and they became fearful. They hid from God in fear. Eating from the tree of the knowledge of good and evil brought them knowledge of separation from God, and thus knowledge of fear.

Fear breaks fellowship with God. As Christians, we are inseparably united with Christ as one spirit with Him. Our fellowship with Him can be broken, however, when we allow things to come into our lives, thoughts, minds, or attitudes that are contrary to the Word and the Spirit of God. These things cause a type of separation from God, and the result is fear. Before we were born again we had many reasons to fear. As believers, though, our separation from God has been removed. Jesus took it away at the cross, and we are now joined with Him. Fear not.

Another consequence of fear is that it activates satan. Just as faith pleases God and brings His action into our lives and circumstances, so fear activates satan. Fear is the opposite of faith. In a way, fear is faith in the devil. Satan puts doubts and fearful thoughts and ideas in our minds, and we believe them. No mental exercise in our own strength can drive out fear. Only being confident of who we are in Jesus and planting His Word deep in our hearts and lives can do it. Fear is not of God. Jesus has set us free from fear.

Faith drives out fear. There are many illustrations of this truth in Scripture. Consider the case of Jairus, the synagogue leader. His story is found in Mark 5:22-43 and Luke 8:41-56. Jairus came to Jesus and asked Him to heal his daughter, who was dying. While on the way to Jairus' house, Jesus healed a woman who had been hemorrhaging for 12 years. This was certainly a faith-builder for Jairus. Then

Jairus received the news that his daughter was dead. Jesus' first words to him were, "Don't be afraid." If Jairus believed, his daughter would be healed. Jairus' faith drove out his fear, and his daughter was brought back to life.

Another example is found in Second Kings 4:8-37. A Shunammite woman showed hospitality to the prophet Elisha by providing him a room to stay in whenever he traveled that way. In fulfillment of Elisha's prophecy, she was blessed with a son. When the young boy died suddenly, his mother refused to succumb to fear. She laid the child on the bed in Elisha's room, said nothing to her husband or the servants—only that it was all right—and took off immediately with haste to find the prophet. In other words, no negative expressions of fear came from her mouth, only words of faith: "Everything is all right." She believed in Elisha's anointing as a man of God. After all, had he not prophesied the birth of her boy and would he not be the one to help her now? It was common for unusual things to happen through the men of God, and she believed that her promised son would be brought back to life again. The woman's faith in God's power to heal drove out any fear she had for her son, and he was restored to her.

Feeding our minds and spirits on the Word of God is a great antidote to fear. Consider these promises:

I took you from the ends of the earth, from its farthest corners I called you. I said, "You are My servant"; I have chosen you and have not rejected you. So do not fear, for I am with you; do not be dismayed, for I am your God. I will strengthen you and help you; I will uphold you with My righteous right hand. All who rage against you will surely be ashamed and disgraced; those who oppose you will be as nothing and perish. Though you search for your enemies, you will not find them. Those who wage war against you will be as nothing at all. For I am the Lord, your God, who takes hold of your right hand and says to you, Do not fear; I will help you (Isaiah 41:9-13).

But now, this is what the Lord says—He who created you, O Jacob, He who formed you, O Israel: "Fear not, for I have redeemed you; I have summoned you by name; you are Mine. When you pass through the waters, I will be with you; and when you pass through the rivers, they will not sweep over you. When you walk through the fire, you will not be burned; the flames will not set you ablaze" (Isaiah 43:1-2).

But whoever listens to me [wisdom] *will live in safety and be at ease, without fear of harm* (Proverbs 1:33).

For God did not give us a spirit of timidity, but a spirit of power, of love and of self-discipline (2 Timothy 1:7).

I will extol the Lord at all times; His praise will always be on my lips. My soul will boast in the Lord; let the afflicted hear and rejoice. Glorify the Lord with me; let us exalt His name together. I sought the Lord, and He answered me; He delivered me from all my fears (Psalm 34:1-4).

Fret Not

What are the things you worry about the most? What things irritate you? What are your pet peeves? All sorts of things cause us to fret and worry: things at home, things at work, things about our spouses or our children, things in daily life. Whatever they are, they chew away at us until we are edgy and irritable. Most of us recognize that fretting, worrying, and getting upset and irritated serve no useful purpose, yet we still fall into doing them.

How well I remember the early years of discovering the adventures and joys of learning about the Holy Spirit. In those days I was far more "spiritual" than my dear husband (my opinion only). I embarked on my "toilet tank ministry." Some of you reading this have one too, so you can really relate. I faithfully removed the *Reader's Digest* and *Popular Mechanics* from the "reading room" and replaced them with the latest tracts, Christian periodicals, and "good" books. He would have no choice but to read them and discover what I was so excited about. You might say I fretted when I found them lying on the floor unread and the latest mystery novel in their place.

I was really thrilled when Bill agreed to accompany me, a friend of mine, and her husband, to a weekend conference on spiritual growth. My favorite speakers were on the program, and my friend and I were there to serve, help with the registrations and book table, and soak up any anointing that might be pouring out. Our husbands agreed to usher after some mild manipulation. We thought, "Super, that means they will have to be at the meetings." They were such rascals, though, disappearing as soon as the program began, going out behind the building to sit, talk, and have a smoke. (Fret not, they're free of that vice now.)

Well, the "straw that broke the camel's back" happened the final day of the conference. The afternoon speaker was exceptional, with a message that I wanted my husband to hear, so I worked on him all morning, getting him to promise to be at the meeting. I maneuvered to get both of us a front row seat and planned to meet him there when the service began, but when the time came, he was nowhere in sight. I stewed away, fretted, fussed, felt resentment and anger (godly qualities of a Spirit-filled woman, right?). Where was he? I stomped out, went around the building, through the park, and all over the place, but I couldn't find him. As a last resort, I went to our hotel room. There he was, as happy as if he was in his right mind, lying on the bed in his underwear, watching the football game. What a variety of emotions I experienced! I was speechless (a miracle for me) and returned to the meeting, sitting at the back in a secluded corner, oozing out some tears of self-pity.

That day I began a process of learning to "fret not" and to release Bill into the hands of a faithful God, instead of trying to manipulate him. I realized that we were both individuals accountable for our own walk with the Lord and that my only responsibility was to be a caring, loving wife as I got on with the things of the Kingdom in whatever sphere God was calling me to. It's amazing how spouses can change when we get off their backs. Fretting, worrying, and manipulating accomplishes nothing; accepting and releasing is the answer. My husband is the dearest, most enjoyable person to be with, supporting me totally in the ministry I'm called to, and walking in his own quiet, personal way with his Lord.

In Philippians 4:6-7 Paul says:

Do not be anxious about anything, but in everything, by prayer and petition, with thanksgiving, present your requests to God. And the peace of God, which transcends all understanding, will guard your hearts and your minds in Christ Jesus.

He says not to worry about anything. It's a command. All of us have the freedom to choose whether or not to worry. Instead of worrying, we should take everything to God with a thankful and confident heart. When we do, God's peace, an inner tranquillity beyond human understanding and the opposite of worry, will fill our hearts and minds.

Peter gives similar counsel in First Peter 5:7: "Cast all your anxiety on Him because He cares for you." God cares about us and wants us to give to Him all our concerns and burdens.

What effect does worrying have on us? First of all, it steals the Word from our hearts. If we are worrying about something, we cannot focus on the Word of God. Second, it prevents us from being fruitful in the Spirit; and third, it distracts us from the things of God. The Word of God and the life of the Spirit cannot produce healthy spiritual fruit in us if we are preoccupied with the worries and cares of life. The river of life we are supposed to release into our world gets dammed up by the burdens, anxieties, and distractions of daily living.

Jesus illustrated this in His parable about the sower and the seed (see Mt. 13:3-9; Mk. 4:3-9; Lk. 8:5-8). Some of the seed fell among thorns that grew up and choked the plants, preventing fruitfulness. The thorns represent the cares and anxieties of the world, the distractions of this age, the pleasures, delights, glamour, and deceitfulness of riches, and the craving for things. These thorns creep in and choke and suffocate the Word sown in us and we become fruitless.

How many people do you know whose every conversation seems to be fret, fret, fret, and worry, worry, worry? They have a problem that they just turn over and over until they can't talk or think about anything else. Are you like that? Are you damming up the river of life in you by allowing the cares and anxieties of the world to overwhelm you and choke off the Word of God? Worrying is a tough habit to break, but it can be done in the power of God.

Don't ask God for the grace to bear your burdens. He doesn't want you to do that. He wants you to give your burdens to Him. Psalm 55:22 says, "Cast your cares on the Lord and He will sustain you; He will never let the righteous fall." That is a wonderful promise for all of us. He will sustain us and never let us fall as we roll our burdens onto Him and let Him carry them. We are not strong enough to bear our burdens; some of them will crush us. If we insist on trying, we will not experience the fullness of His promise in that verse.

Psalm 37 gives the remedy for fretting:

__Do not fret__ because of evil men or be envious of those who do wrong; for like the grass they will soon wither, like green plants they will soon die away. __Trust in the Lord and do good__; dwell in the land and enjoy safe pasture. __Delight yourself in the Lord__ and He will give you the desires of your heart. __Commit your way to the Lord__; trust in Him and He will do this: He will make your righteousness shine like the dawn, the justice of your cause like the noonday sun. __Be still before the Lord and wait patiently for Him__; do not fret when men succeed in their ways, when they carry out their wicked schemes. __Refrain from anger and turn from wrath__; do not fret—it leads only to evil (Psalm 37:1-8).

The command is given in verse 1, "Do not fret." The solution is found in verses 3, 4, 5, and 7; we are to: trust in the Lord, delight in Him, commit our ways to Him, and be still and wait patiently for Him. It is amazing what the Lord can do with our problems once He has them, but as long as we hold onto them, we will never know what that is. Our daily lives will simply continue on defeated, fruitless, and frustrated.

It is wonderful to know that we can roll our anxieties on Him, but we have to believe that He is able to do what He says He will do. Too often we don't give Him the chance. If we do give something over to Him, many times we become impatient if the circumstance doesn't change right away. Then we grab it back and start chewing on it again and never come into freedom. Let's take Him at His Word. Let's not fret or worry, but cast all our cares on Him who cares for us, and allow Him to deliver us, sustain us, and produce healthy fruit in us. Let's stop damming up the river.

Faint Not

The third needed negative is "faint not." In other words, hang in there. Don't give up. Don't relax your effort toward God. Don't slack off. Paul said, "I have fought the good fight, I have finished the race, I have kept the faith" (2 Tim. 4:7).

It is very true that we reap what we sow. When we plant a garden we don't get a crop right away. Are we such "instant mashed potato" types that we expect quick answers to all our prayers? We may be great in the short sprint, but how are we in the long race?

Three examples from the Old Testament will help us understand this principle of patience and perseverance.

Daniel 10 describes a frightening and puzzling vision that Daniel had. He fasted and prayed and pleaded for three weeks for God to give him an answer. Three times a day for three weeks he prayed and waited and never gave up. Finally, an angel appeared and explained that Daniel's prayers had been heard on the first day, but spiritual opposition from the enemy had prevented the angel from coming to him sooner. What if Daniel had given up after a week and a half? He persevered with patience and the answer came.

Look at Abraham. Did he relax his effort toward God? Did he faint? He believed God's promise that he would have a son in his old age, and waited a quarter of a century for that promise to be fulfilled. He was already an old man when the promise was made, and at the age of 100, when it looked as if there was no way on God's green earth that anything like that could happen, lo and behold, Isaac was born. Abraham fainted not at God's promise. It was not just a temporary thing, either. Genesis records that after Isaac, Abraham had other children also (see Gen. 25:1-2).

First Kings 18:19-46 records the story of Elijah and the prophets of Baal on Mount Carmel. Rain had not fallen in the land for three years, in fulfillment of a pronouncement Elijah had made at God's direction. The dramatic contest on Mount Carmel ended with God's consuming Elijah's water-drenched sacrifice, and the subsequent execution of the prophets of Baal. Then Elijah, again at God's direction, prophesied that rain would fall for the first time in three years. Elijah waited in intercession for a long time under clear blue skies. Seven times he sent his servant to check the sky for rain clouds. Finally, after the seventh time, the servant reported seeing a small cloud like a man's hand. Then the rain came in torrents. Elijah hung in there through it all and never gave up. He never doubted the word of the Lord.

Sometimes running the race can become stale and tiring. How many times have we prayed about a situation but, when we don't see the answer right away, become indifferent about it and miss the answer when it was right around the corner? Thanks be to God who gives us the victory and makes us conquerors through our Lord Jesus Christ! The answer is right around the corner and that's where we need to walk. Faint not, knowing that the answer is waiting to be revealed.

But thanks be to God! He gives us the victory through our Lord Jesus Christ. Therefore, my dear brothers, stand firm. Let nothing move you. Always give yourselves fully to the work of the Lord, because you know that your labor in the Lord is not in vain (1 Corinthians 15:57-58).

Let us not become weary in doing good, for at the proper time we will reap a harvest if we do not give up (Galatians 6:9)

Hang in there. The harvest is sure, the rewards certain—if we don't give up.

Forsake Not

The fourth needed negative is "forsake not." The key verse for this one is Hebrews 10:25:

Not forsaking or neglecting to assemble together [as believers], as is the habit of some people, but admonishing (warning, urging, and encouraging) one another, and all the more faithfully as you see the day approaching (AMP).

So often we hear people say, "I can be a good Christian and praise God out there on the golf course at 10 o'clock in the

morning. I don't have to go to church to be a Christian."
Maybe not, but none of us can be fruitful, growing, maturing, Spirit-filled believers without being regular and active
in church. Why? We need our church family in order to
admonish, warn, urge, and encourage us. Those things are
hard to do when you are by yourself.

Meeting together regularly is vital if we are to be
equipped for ministry. The fivefold ministry in Ephesians
4:11 of apostles, prophets, evangelists, pastors, and teachers
is given for the whole Body of Christ. As believers, we each
have our places, we each have our gifts, and we each have
ministries God has called us to. We must not forsake meeting together in order that we may be equipped by the
"body" gifts that are given to the Church. Then we can
grow up into maturity and find our places in the Body of
Christ.

We need to meet together regularly so that we may bear
one another's burdens. Jesus wants us to care for one another in this way. Galatians 6:2 says, "Carry each other's
burdens, and in this way you will fulfill the law of Christ."
Bearing one another's burdens does not mean we carry everyone's load, but that we restore other individuals in grace,
mercy, and compassion. We don't rap them over the head or
stand in judgment over them. I've heard it said that Christians are the only people who bury their wounded. Think
about that. Someone in the fellowship makes a mistake or
slips into sin, and we let him fall on his face. No, we are to
lovingly, gently, and tenderly restore one another when we
stumble.

Meeting together regularly is important so that we may confess our faults one to another. It is a difficult and humbling

experience, but what freedom comes! Consider James 5:16: "Therefore confess your sins to each other and pray for each other so that you may be healed. The prayer of a righteous man is powerful and effective."

We need to meet together regularly so we can stand firm and united in Christ against the enemy and deception.

Whatever happens, conduct yourselves in a manner worthy of the gospel of Christ. Then, whether I come and see you or only hear about you in my absence, I will know that you stand firm in one spirit, contending as one man for the faith of the gospel without being frightened in any way by those who oppose you. This is a sign to them that they will be destroyed, but that you will be saved—and that by God (Philippians 1:27-28).

We must stand together in unity with one mind and purpose, constant and fearless, and harmonious, with no contentious factions. It is also vital that we watch together to prevent a wolf of divisiveness in the Body that could separate and destroy us. "Divide and conquer" is one of satan's favorite and most successful strategies.

Let us not forsake meeting together regularly. We need each other.

Forget Not

The fifth needed negative is "forget not." Forget not what? Forget not all His benefits. Forget not all His promises. We need to feed regularly on the Word of God and take it to heart so we can remember it and use it in our daily lives. Look at Psalm 103:

Praise the Lord, O my soul; all my inmost being, praise His holy name. Praise the Lord, O my soul,

*and **forget not** all His benefits—who forgives all your
sins and heals all your diseases, who redeems your
life from the pit and crowns you with love and compassion, who satisfies your desires with good things
so that your youth is renewed like the eagle's. ... He
does not treat us as our sins deserve or repay us according to our iniquities. For as high as the heavens
are above the earth, so great is His love for those who
fear Him; as far as the east is from the west, so far
has He removed our transgressions from us* (Psalm
103:1-5,10-12).

Do you want to know the sure cure for depression?
Praise the Lord. That's it. Praise the Lord. Once you begin
praising and glorifying the Lord, there is no way you can
stay down and depressed for very long. Psalm 105:1-8 contains an excellent pattern for this. If you will follow it, "do
it," and make it personal, you will be out of your depression
and into God's presence so fast it will make your head
swim. Please "do" the following, not simply read it!

***Give thanks to the Lord, call on His name; make
known** among the nations **what He has done. Sing to
Him, sing praise to Him; tell of all His wonderful
acts. Glory in His holy name;** let the hearts of those
who seek the Lord rejoice. Look to the Lord and His
strength; seek His face always. **Remember the wonders He has done**, His miracles, and the judgments
He pronounced, O descendants of Abraham His servant, O sons of Jacob, His chosen ones. He is the
Lord our God; His judgments are in all the earth. He
remembers His covenant forever, the word He commanded, for a thousand generations* (Psalm 105:1-8).

So, there we have them, the five needed negatives: fear not, fret not, faint not, forsake not, and forget not. All of them are biblical principles and vital to our health and welfare as children of the Kingdom. As we move forward to become releasers of life, we will need these principles to help us face the inevitable discouragements that will come our way.

Chapter 9

Overcoming Discouragement

Discouragement is one of the most crippling enemies we face in life. Not one of us is safe from it. It springs up in the most unlikely places at the most unexpected times and knocks us flat on our backs. It beats us down, robs us of joy and confidence, and leaves us bruised and hurting. The walking wounded are all around us—people who are battered and scarred, their hopes and dreams dashed to pieces on the cruel rocks of discouragement.

Unfortunately, the same condition exists for many of us in the Church. Whenever we begin walking in the Spirit and seeking the way of the Lord, whether as a body of believers or as individuals, we become targets of satan's special attention. The enemy knows that if he can discourage us to the point of giving up, he will have won a victory almost as great as if we had never been saved. When the rest of the world looks at Christians and sees us stumbling along in defeat, fear, strife, intimidation, and self-consciousness, what in us would they want? They would say, "Why, they are no different from us."

Releasing life into the Body of Christ and the world involves learning to overcome discouragement. That means understanding where it comes from and knowing how to deal with it.

Three Sources of Discouragement

One major source of discouragement is **outward circumstances**. When things get tough and negative situations grab our attention, if we're not careful, we'll begin to dwell on them and be consumed by them. When all hell is breaking loose and it seems there is no way out, that's when discouragement comes roaring in.

A classic example is of the nation of Israel soon after the exodus. Many of those folks were walking, breathing bags of discouragement. They could not take their eyes or minds off their lousy circumstances: barren wilderness, scarcity of food, lack of water, and the daily hardships of nomadic life. They quickly and repeatedly forgot the mercies and power and deliverance of God on their behalf. There they were at the Red Sea, with the water before them, the Egyptians behind them, and nowhere to go. They griped and complained to Moses, beginning a pattern that repeated itself time and again despite God's deliverance and continual provision for their needs.

At the very border of Canaan not long after the parting of the sea, a final act of rebellion deprived that generation of the opportunity to enter and occupy the land God had promised. He had spoken His word. All they had to do was go in and possess what was already theirs. Twelve chosen men went in to check things out. They literally saw the promise and touched it, but ten of them had no room in their hearts to really believe. Based on outward circumstances, they returned with a bad report that infected the faith of the whole community: "Too many powerful people...too many walled cities...too many giants...too strong for us...they'll eat us alive...we'll be killed, our wives and children captured...we see ourselves as grass-hoppers...we are not able." Only two returned with reports of faith, and almost got murdered because of it. As a result, the Israelites wandered around outside the land for 40 years, all because discouragement over their outward circumstances overwhelmed their faith and confidence in God.

Outward circumstances can be very deceptive. In Second Kings chapter 6, a foreign army under the king of Aram surrounded the city of Dothan in order to capture the prophet Elisha. When Elisha's servant saw the massive forces, he was frightened. The situation looked very bad. Elisha saw beyond the circumstances. He knew that God was on his side, protecting them. He said to his servant, "Those who are with us are more than those who are with them" (2 Kings 6:16b). Elisha prayed, and the servant's eyes were opened to see the angelic hosts that had been there all along surrounding and protecting them. When we focus on outward circumstances, we cannot see the resources that God has made available to us. Seeing things as they really are, through spiritual eyes, puts temporal circumstances in proper perspective.

Discouragement over circumstances depends on your perspective. It can be overcome through praise and worship. Acts 16:12-40 tells of Paul and Silas in Philippi. They had been preaching and ministering for several weeks, dogged at every step by a young slave girl who was possessed by a demonic spirit of divination. They delivered her from that, depriving her owners of the income they received from her "gift." This landed Paul and Silas in prison, flat on their backs with their feet in the stocks and rats running around everywhere. In the middle of the night they were praising God and singing when an earthquake shook the place, and the chains of every prisoner there came loose. Before the night was over, the jailer and his entire household had been brought to Christ. Praise and worship will not always lead to such a miraculous deliverance from bad circumstances, but praise and worship will put those circumstances in a new light, enabling us to view them from God's perspective.

A second source of discouragement is **things we hear that are not of God**. Faith comes by hearing, and hearing, and hearing the Word of God. In a similar way fear comes by hearing, and hearing, and hearing that which is not of God. Jesus said in Mark 4:24, "Consider carefully what you hear....With the measure you use, it will be measured to you—and even more." So, the more we expose ourselves to the things of God, hearing His Word and listening to His Spirit, the more we will understand, the more we will be encouraged, and the more we will be built up in strength and faith.

On the other hand, if we fill our minds with ungodly attitudes, worldly philosophies, negativism, and other things contrary to the Word of God, then that is what will grow strong in us, and fear and discouragement are sure to follow. Either we listen to and abide by God's Word, growing strong in faith; or we hear and heed the lies, growing strong in fear.

The third source of discouragement is the **foolish and ignorant words that come out of our own mouths**—those falsely humble or self-defeating things that are contrary to God's desires for us. Such things as "I'll never succeed," or

"I'm really not worth much," or "God could never use me," or "This one is too big for Him to handle," or "This is too small for God to bother with," and the like, are sure-fire discouragement builders. We need to heed Proverbs 18:21: "The tongue has the power of life and death, and those who love it will eat its fruit."

So **looking at the wrong things, listening to the wrong things**, and **saying the wrong things** open the door for discouragement to rush in and overwhelm us. If we set our hearts and minds on things above rather than on earthly things (see Col. 3:1-2), we can draw on the inexhaustible spiritual resources of God to keep discouragement at bay.

Paul's "Thorn in the Flesh"—Discouragement Overcome

If ever there was a candidate for discouragement, it was the apostle Paul. He faced incredible hardships everywhere he went. Danger and difficulty dogged his every step. Yet, he rose above it all and God used him mightily. How did he do it? How did Paul defeat discouragement? He learned how to see from a heavenly perspective and to depend on heavenly power. He revealed some of his insight in his second letter to the Corinthians:

To keep me from becoming conceited because of these surpassingly great revelations, there was given me a thorn in my flesh, a messenger of Satan, to torment me. Three times I pleaded with the Lord to take it away from me. But He said to me, "My grace is sufficient for you, for My power is made perfect in weakness." Therefore I will boast all the more gladly about my weaknesses, so that Christ's power may rest on me. That is why, for Christ's sake, I delight in

*weaknesses, in insults, in hardships, in persecutions,
in difficulties. For when I am weak, then I am strong*
(2 Corinthians 12:7-10).

Earlier in the chapter Paul referred to a "man in Christ"
who was caught up to "the third heaven" where he heard
"inexpressible things." Most Bible scholars agree that Paul
was referring to himself. He was the recipient of many great
and glorious revelations from God. Because of the greatness of those revelations, Paul was given a "thorn in the
flesh" to keep him humble and dependent on God. For a
long time he had prayed for God to remove it, but when he
understood God's purpose, to display His power through
Paul's weakness, Paul was able to boast and even rejoice in
his weakness. How's that for a positive outlook on negative
circumstances?

The exact nature of Paul's thorn in the flesh has been de-
bated for centuries. To comprehend his insight on dealing
with discouragement, we need to understand what his thorn
was. The most common thought is that Paul's thorn was
some kind of physical ailment, perhaps a problem with his
eyes. He refers in Galatians 4:14-15 to his "illness" and that
the Galatians would have torn out their own eyes and given
them to him if they could have, and in Galatians 6:11 he
mentions the "large letters" he uses when he writes to them
in his own hand. Other scholars have suggested malaria or
some other chronic debilitating condition.

However, there is **no** scriptural evidence linking Paul's
illness in Galatians with his thorn in the flesh. When Paul
uses the word **weaknesses** in Second Corinthians 12:10 he
is not referring to sickness and disease, but to ignorance and
inability. He will glory in his ignorance and inability so that

the power of God will rest on him and be magnified in Paul's weakness.

As a Pharisee thoroughly trained and knowledgeable in the Hebrew Scriptures, Paul had a very deliberate and specific reason for using the words "thorn in the flesh." The phrase occurs in Numbers 33:55 as the Israelites are preparing to enter and conquer the land of Canaan. They are warned to completely drive out the pagan inhabitants of the land, otherwise they will become "...barbs in your eyes and thorns in your sides. They will give you trouble in the land where you will live." Joshua 23:13 and Ezekiel 2:6 both use the word **thorns** in reference to hostile or rebellious people.

Paul says that his thorn was "a messenger of Satan, to torment me." The Greek word for "torment," *kolaphizo*, means "to rap with the fist" or "buffet," and is derived from a word that means to chastise or punish. Sickness and disease do not buffet or chastise. Buffeting is like a boat moored to a dock with waves rolling in from a passing vessel or a storm, banging it repeatedly into the pier—bang, bang, bang. It is like a person being beaten repeatedly on the head and face. Time after time there came into Paul's life circumstances that buffeted him wherever he went, whatever he did.

What does this have to do with discouragement? Paul asked the Lord to remove the thorn. The Lord responded by saying, in effect, "Come on, Paul, you know who you are in Me, and the power that resides within you. My grace and My mercy are going to carry you through. Come on, Paul, remember who you are." I think that is His message to us too: "Come on, Church, remember who you are in the midst of buffeting."

I believe Paul's thorn in the flesh were messengers (*angelos* in the Greek), demonic spirits sent from the enemy. These demon spirits motivated the Judaizers, Jewish professing believers who were very legalistic and who taught that Gentiles had to become Jews and submit to the Jewish Law in order to become Christians. These men followed Paul wherever he went, and tried to destroy and pull down the ministry of the Word of God.

Paul was buffeted in ways that would bring any one of us into deep discouragement. Look at some of the things he endured. The Jews attempted to kill him right after his conversion. He was hindered in joining the Christians. He was opposed by satan. He was opposed by Jews in a mob. He was kicked out of Antioch and Pisidia. He was mobbed and expelled from Iconium. He fled to Lystra and Derbe where he was stoned and left for dead. He disputed continually with false brethren. He was beaten and jailed in Philippi. He was mobbed and expelled from Thessalonica. He was mobbed and expelled from Berea. He was mobbed at Corinth and Ephesus. There was a plot against his life by the Jews. He was seized by the Jews, tried in court five times, and suffered other hardships. Wouldn't you call this a little discouraging?

As if those were not enough, look at the list he gives in Second Corinthians 11:23-28:

...I have worked much harder, been in prison more frequently, been flogged more severely, and been exposed to death again and again. Five times I received from the Jews the forty lashes minus one. Three times I was beaten with rods, once I was stoned, three times I was shipwrecked, I spent a night and a day in the open sea, I have been constantly on the move. I have

been in danger from rivers, in danger from bandits, in danger from my own countrymen, in danger from Gentiles; in danger in the city, in danger in the country, in danger at sea; and in danger from false brothers. I have labored and toiled and have often gone without sleep; I have known hunger and thirst and have often gone without food; I have been cold and naked. Besides everything else, I face daily the pressure of my concern for all the churches (2 Corinthians 11:23-28).

Through it all Paul persevered and prevailed through the presence and power of God in his life. Once, when he was reminding Timothy of all the persecutions and hardships he had endured, he said, "...Yet the Lord rescued me from all of them" (2 Tim. 3:11). In the very next verse he stated that anyone who wished to live a godly life in Christ would suffer persecution. Paul viewed his sufferings in the light of God's purpose. He overcame circumstances that would normally destroy anyone. God's power was made perfect, or put on maximum display, in Paul's weakness. When Paul in weakness withstood insurmountable odds, there could be no doubt of the presence and power of God in his life for all to see. Paul's heavenly perspective enabled him to overcome discouragement.

Scriptural Encouragement

Trouble and difficulty are just facts of life on good old terra firma in a fallen world system. In John 16:33 Jesus said, "I have told you these things, so that in Me you may have peace. In this world you will have trouble. But take heart! I have overcome the world." There will be trouble, but He wants us to know at the same time that His peace and overcoming power are available to us. He has overcome the world and deprived it of its power to harm. For us to stand firm in discouraging circumstances, we must be completely dependent on Him. It is a lifestyle of habitual turning to Him, not just screaming for help when we're in trouble. If we don't turn to Him day by day and intimately know His heart, His will, and His purposes, how are we ever going to find them when all hell breaks loose and we **really** need Him?

Faith comes by hearing, and hearing, and hearing the Word of God. If we sow the Word in our hearts, it will come back to us when we need it. There are hundreds of promises and encouragements in God's Word, and I want to share a few of them with you, just to whet your appetite. Let me encourage you to go digging and discover others for yourself. We can all take encouragement from these:

You, dear children, are from God and have overcome them, because the one who is in you is greater than the one who is in the world (1 John 4:4).

For God did not give us a spirit of timidity, but a spirit of power, of love and of self-discipline (2 Timothy 1:7).

I can do everything through Him who gives me strength (Philippians 4:13).

What, then, shall we say in response to this? If God is for us, who can be against us? ... For I am convinced that neither death nor life, neither angels nor demons, neither the present nor the future, nor any powers, neither height nor depth, nor anything else in all creation, will be able to separate us from the love of God that is in Christ Jesus our Lord (Roman 8:31,38-39).

You will keep in perfect peace him whose mind is steadfast, because he trusts in You (Isaiah 26:3).

Trust in the Lord with all your heart and lean not on your own understanding; in all your ways acknowledge Him, and He will make your paths straight (Proverbs 3:5-6).

With God we will gain the victory, and He will trample down our enemies (Psalm 60:12).

The Lord is my light and my salvation—whom shall I fear? The Lord is the stronghold of my life—of whom shall I be afraid? ...Wait for the Lord; be strong and take heart and wait for the Lord (Psalm 27:1,14).

For surely, O Lord, you bless the righteous; you surround them with your favor as with a shield (Psalm 5:12).

Persistence Pays Off

One of the most effective ways to overcome discouragement is through persistence. Very simply, never give up. This is where "faint not" comes into play (see Chapter 8). Paul said, "...one thing I do: Forgetting what is behind and straining toward what is ahead, I press on toward the goal..." (Phil. 3:13-14). Persistence means to continue steadfastly in spite of opposition; to be insistent and tenacious like a pit bull.

There are many biblical examples of such persistence. Let's look at a couple in detail. These are faith taking action. Faith hears and faith sees, but faith takes action too. Mark recorded the first example in chapter 10 of his Gospel:

Then they came to Jericho. As Jesus and His disciples, together with a large crowd, were leaving the city, a blind man, Bartimaeus (that is, the Son of Ti-maeus), was sitting by the roadside begging. When he heard that it was Jesus of Nazareth, he began to shout, "Jesus, Son of David, have mercy on me!" Many rebuked him and told him to be quiet, but he shouted all the more, "Son of David, have mercy on me!" Jesus stopped and said, "Call him." So they called to the blind man, "Cheer up! On your feet! He's calling you." Throwing his cloak aside, he jumped to his feet and came to Jesus. "What do you want Me to do for you?" Jesus asked him. The blind man said, "Rabbi, I want to see." "Go," said Jesus, "your faith has healed you." Immediately he received his sight and followed Jesus along the road (Mark 10:46-52).

Blind Bartimaeus sat by the roadside day after day. His only livelihood was begging. He listened a lot, though, and no doubt had heard about Jesus long before He came along that road outside Jericho. Bartimaeus had heard of the miracles and the healings. He knew about the remarkable rabbi from Galilee. What hope, though, did he have of ever meeting Jesus?

One day Bartimaeus heard a large crowd coming down the road. Upon learning it was Jesus, Bartimaeus put his faith into action. He was determined not to let this opportunity escape. He began shouting for Jesus to have mercy on him. The context of the verb means "right now." "Jesus, have mercy on me right now."

Many in the crowd rebuked Bartimaeus and told him to be quiet. Did you notice his reaction? Instead of listening to the opposition, to those who tried to shut him up, he continued to shout, but even louder than before. Bartimaeus was not about to give up!

This is where persistence paid off. Jesus heard Bartimaeus' cry, stopped, and called to him. Some of those around Bartimaeus told him to cheer up because Jesus was calling him. (Were these some of the same ones who had tried to shut him up before?) Look at the eagerness and confidence of this man. Mark says that Bartimaeus **threw his cloak aside** and **jumped to his feet** to go to Jesus. Can't you just picture him pressing his way through the crowd, groping with his hands, following Jesus' voice, perhaps being led by a friend? Bartimaeus could not get to Jesus quickly enough!

When Bartimaeus stood before Jesus, Jesus asked him, "What do you want Me to do for you?" That question was full of love and compassion. He gave Bartimaeus the chance to state specifically what he wanted. Jesus does the same for us. He wants us to be specific.

Bartimaeus was bold in his reply. "Rabbi, I want to see." Jesus appreciates boldness and confidence when we approach Him. They are signs of faith. They indicate that we really believe that He can and will respond.

Jesus honored Bartimaeus' faith and granted his request. "Go, your faith has healed you." Bartimaeus responded by immediately following Jesus on the road. His life and future were changed forever.

The truly wonderful thing in this story is the faith displayed by Bartimaeus. It was not that he simply cried out persistently to Jesus for healing. Jesus knew by Bartimaeus' actions that he fully expected to receive his healing. Bartimaeus gave a strong signal when he threw off his beggar's cloak and left it behind. Bartimaeus' beggar's cloak was his everything. He kept his meager possessions in its pockets. He used it as a tent for shelter. It was his identification badge, his license to beg. When Bartimaeus stood up to go to Jesus, he threw off his beggar's cloak because he knew he would never need it again. He was never going to be a beggar again. He knew it beyond a shadow of a doubt. He left his blind beggar's life behind him as he rushed to Jesus in faith to receive his healing. His persistence brought him to Jesus. His faith brought him his sight. Persistence paid off.

An Immensely Discouraging Circumstance Changed

One of the most meaningful accounts of faith and persistence, in my opinion, is the story in Mark 5:25-34 of the woman who had been hemorrhaging for 12 years. We relate to her distress to some extent, but I wonder how well we really understand her situation as it was. Her physical condition must have been pathetic after bleeding for 12 years. Most of us couldn't put up with it for more than a couple of months, if that. She was probably very low in iron and energy, and most likely weak and continually tired. She had been to doctor after doctor with no change in her condition. The Bible says she had spent all that she had seeking "medical" help.

According to *Dake's Annotated Reference Bible*, she would have suffered greatly with these various treatments, which would have included such things as drinking bitter herbs, inhaling the fumes from burning new grape leaves, being subjected to sudden fright (I guess that was supposed to startle it out of her), and having to squat over certain ditches for considerable periods of time.[1] Instead of getting better, she got worse. She was considered unclean—like a leper—and was forbidden to appear in public, especially where there were men present. She was drained, hopeless, degraded, weak, in pain, broke, rejected, and very discouraged.

One day, she heard about Jesus. Perhaps someone passing by her house told of the miracles and wonders happening in the land: the blind seeing, the deaf hearing, the lame running and jumping, the demons being cast out. Remember, faith comes by hearing. She heard He was coming to town, and she got the idea that if she could get near enough to Him to touch the hem of His prayer shawl, she would be healed. The Bible doesn't say where she actually lived. Did she live just one street over from the main one, or did she live three miles outside of town? How far did she have to walk?

Faith and persistence rose up in her and in spite of the prohibitions about being in public, she set out in her weakened state to meet Jesus. She must have been trembling inside and fearful of being exposed. Imagine her thoughts when she arrived near the street, only to find that the crowd was so thick one could hardly move. Drained of energy and strength, something rose up within her, enabling her to push and squeeze and wiggle around the arms and legs and bodies until she got close enough to Him. Straining with all the strength she could muster, she reached out and touched His garment. As soon as she did so, the flow of blood stopped, and she felt in her body that she was healed. At the same time, Jesus felt the healing power go out from Him and knew that someone had drawn it from Him by faith. There was no reproach from Him that she had "helped herself," only acceptance and encouragement.

No matter what our circumstances are, our Lord is the one who turns discouragement into hope, captivity into freedom, and brokenness into wholeness. He's the one who is able to release us from everything that would entangle or incapacitate us, setting us free to move on in liberty.

Endnotes

1. Finis Jennings Dake, *Dake's Annotated Reference Bible* (Atlanta, GA: Dake Bible Sales, Inc., 1961, 1963).

Chapter 10

Snares and Hobbles

And they bring unto Him one that was deaf, and had an impediment in his speech; and they beseech Him to put His hand upon him. And He took him aside from the multitude, and put His fingers into his ears, and He spit, and touched his tongue; and looking up to heaven, He sighed, and saith unto him, Ephphatha, that is, Be opened. And straightway his ears were opened, and the string of his tongue was loosed, and he spake plain (Mark 7:32-35 KJV).

Years ago, when I worked as a nurse in labor and delivery, part of the initial examination of a newborn was to check for a condition called "tongue-tie." This is when the membrane underneath the tongue attaches itself to the front of the mouth, preventing the tongue from moving freely. In this condition the child cannot nurse or speak properly. The doctor would snip the membrane with a pair of small, sharp scissors, loosening the string of the baby's tongue.

When I read the account of the healing of the deaf man, and that "the string of his tongue was loosed," I realized,

"Wow, the guy was not mute; he was tongue-tied. He couldn't talk right." That's the trouble with many of us: we're tongue-tied as Christians, and ensnared and hobbled in lots of other ways too.

Snares entrap, entangle, and incapacitate. Hobbles hamper free movement, as when a calf's legs are hobbled together with a short rope to hold it down for branding. As releasers of life, we must learn how to avoid the snares and cut the hobbles that hinder us from moving on with God, and release others into that same freedom.

The Snare of Fear

As I studied many different types of crippling snares and hobbles in the Bible, I discovered that every one of them was related in some way to fear. Fear is probably the greatest crippler of all. I want to give you a definition of fear in the form of an acrostic. Fear is:

**False
Evidence
Appearing
Real**

Please understand that I don't mean the natural, sensible, God-given, adrenaline-pumping fear, the kind designed to warn us of danger and protect us from harm. The fear I'm talking about is the panicky, crippling, ungodly kind that causes us to believe lies, and that paralyzes us in our walk with God. It seizes us by the throat and fills us with dread and anxiety, until the only thing we want to do is flee. Many, many believers throughout the Body of Christ are in the strangling grip of this kind of fear.

One of the biggest snares is the fear of man. We are so afraid of what others may think, and we are so desperate for their approval. Fear of man makes us feel intimidated and inferior. It tongue-ties us so that we do not speak out about God's grace, goodness, and mercy. We become timid at the thought of talking about the reality of God and what He is doing in the world.

Proverbs 29:25 says, "Fear of man will prove to be a snare, but whoever trusts in the Lord is kept safe." For many years I read and quoted that verse without paying much attention to the second part of it. Certainly it is true that the fear of man is a snare. We experience that all the time. If we stop there, though, we miss such a blessing in the second half of the verse: "whoever trusts in the Lord is kept safe." If we would take that to heart and really believe it and walk by it, our fear of man would disappear.

Remember, "For God did not give us a spirit of timidity, but a spirit of power, of love and of self-discipline" (2 Tim. 1:7). The spirit of fear is a spirit of the world, not of God. The Spirit of God can drive away all our fear, if we will let Him. David said, "I sought the Lord, and He answered me; He delivered me from all my fears" (Ps. 34:4). The key here is seeking the Lord. Too often, when the icy hand of fear grips us, we don't even think of seeking the Lord for deliverance from it. His promise is there for us. All we need to do is reach out in faith and receive it.

The Hobble of Oppression

The first hobble is oppression imposed by others. The Israelites were oppressed and enslaved by the Egyptians for hundreds of years. They were so thoroughly hobbled in their lives and choices that they could barely move. They groaned under their heavy burdens and cried out to God. God heard their cry, and remembered the covenant He had made with their forefathers. (See Exodus 2:23-24.)

Hebrews 11:6 says that without faith it is impossible to please God. God is moved by our faith to, not by our need. God responded to the faith of the Israelites, not to their need for liberation. When the Israelites turned to God in faith, God called Moses and through him led the people into freedom.

It is no different now. Just as the Israelites were under the domination, manipulation, and control of the Egyptians, so today there are scores of people in the Body of Christ who are under the domination, manipulation, and control of others, either openly or subtly. Forced submission to another human being is a binding, crippling thing that is absolutely contrary to the will and purpose of God.

One of God's most precious gifts to mankind is the freedom of choice. He never violates that freedom, even when we use it to reject Him. He is not interested in forced or manipulated relationships. He wants us to relate to Him of our own free will. In the same manner, just as we are created in His image, we must have the same attitude toward others, respecting their free will and not seeking to dominate or control them. To do otherwise violates God's gift and design for every person. It is direct rebellion against Him and His purposes for mankind.

The Hobble of Satan

Many people are hobbled by satan himself into bondage to fear, especially the fear of separation from God and the fear of death. Fear, separation, and death were the fruits of Adam's and Eve's disobedience, and have been the legacy of man ever since. Intimacy and communion with God were destroyed. Jesus has restored that intimacy and communion for us as believers, and we are just now beginning to learn how to walk in them.

If we are in Christ, fear of death has no power over us. Hebrews 2:14-15 says that Jesus shared our humanity "so that by His death He might destroy him who holds the power of death—that is, the devil—and free those who all their lives were held in slavery by their fear of death." Paul writes in Romans 8:15-16, "For you did not receive a spirit that makes you a slave again to fear, but you received the Spirit of sonship. And by Him we cry, 'Abba, Father.' The Spirit Himself testifies with our spirit that we are God's children."

Fear is contrary to God's desire for His children. First John 4:17-18 says:

> In this way, love is made complete among us so that we will have confidence on the day of judgment, because in this world we are like Him. There is no fear in love. But perfect love drives out fear, because fear has to do with punishment. The one who fears is not made perfect in love.

Perfect love drives out fear. Jesus Christ is the embodiment of love. In Him there is no fear. Fear is related to punishment, but there is no punishment, no condemnation, for anyone who is in Christ (see Rom. 8:1). Salvation was poured out on the cross 2,000 years ago. The gift of eternal life and everything that goes with it are ours to accept and receive.

The enemy tries to keep us in ignorance of these truths. He tempts us, and when we fall into sin he robs us of our assurance of who we are in Christ and of our assurance of our salvation. He hobbles us through the fear of doing or saying something that will displease God and break our relationship with Him. We get wrapped up in the dread of never knowing whether we are in or out of God's grace.

This state of affairs is not what God wants for us. He wants us to be sure of our status, to know beyond a shadow of a doubt that we are His:

> *And this is the testimony: God has given us eternal life, and this life is in His Son. He who has the Son has life; he who does not have the Son of God does not have life. I write these things to you who believe in the name of the Son of God so that you may know that you have eternal life* (1 John 5:11-13).

The Hobble of Religion

False religion is a hobble that binds millions of people all over the world in confusion and blindness. One of the most common characteristics of false religion, whatever form it takes, is **legalism**, which is focusing on rules, rituals, regulations, and human effort in order to attain right standing with God. We need to take seriously Paul's admonition in Galatians 5:1: "It is for freedom that Christ has set us free. Stand firm, then, and do not let yourselves be burdened again by a yoke of slavery."

Legalism is sin, pure and simple. The Judaizers, those "thorns" in Paul's flesh, were legalists who insisted that the Christian faith involve strict adherence to the Jewish Law in addition to faith in Christ. Paul fought this heresy tooth and nail throughout his ministry. He emphasized over and over again salvation by grace through faith alone.

As Christians, we do not have a religion. We have Life, a dynamic relationship with the living God. Godliness comes from Christ's living within us through the Holy Spirit, not from obeying some external code of behavior. It is absolutely fruitless for us to attempt to attain righteousness through any list of rules or patterns of behavior. Any such use of legalistic means to try to earn salvation is an absolute distortion of God's truth. Paul tells us in Romans 13:9 that all the commandments are summed up in the one command to love our neighbors as ourselves. Jesus Himself called this the second greatest commandment after that of loving God supremely (see Mk. 12:28-31). Paul continues in the next verse, Romans 13:10, to say that love is the fulfillment of the law. Only the Holy Spirit flourishing in us can fulfill the law in and through us. There is life in the Spirit. There is no life in the law.

The Judaizers criticized Paul's new lifestyle of freedom in Christ. He responded, "I'm free from religious bondage. Why does anyone want me to go back to it?" Likewise, we are free to serve the Lord in any ways that are consistent with His Word, His will, His nature, and His holiness. Let's cut the hobble of legalism and the false trappings of religion and step out into the full freedom of abundant life in Jesus Christ.

The Hobble of Weights That Hinder

Therefore, since we are surrounded by such a great cloud of witnesses, let us throw off everything that hinders and the sin that so easily entangles, and let us run with perseverance the race marked out for us (Hebrews 12:1).

The King James Version says to "lay aside every weight" that hinders. These are the unnecessaries, the complications and distractions that don't add a thing to our lives and our walk with God. They are not necessarily bad in themselves, but they hinder us from focusing on the Lord.

The writer of Hebrews used the metaphor of an athletic foot race. In ancient days, even as now, runners training for races would fasten weights to their ankles to build up strength and speed in their legs. When the time came for the actual contest, the weights came off and the runners raced off unhindered and unencumbered. So the writer says, "Get rid of the weights that hobble you, that hold you back from really running."

There is also the "sin that so easily entangles." Do you have any of those little stinkers, those persistent, nagging problems that just never go away and seem to trip you up all the time? Let's throw them off, lay them aside, and not let them be hindrances and distractions to us. Let's "run with perseverance the race marked out for us."

The Hobble of Tribulation

Satan has many weapons that he uses to attack and beat down God's people. Four of the most effective are tribulation, persecution because of the Word, worldly cares, and worldly desires. Each of these is a dangerous snare and hobble that we must watch out for.

Tribulation literally means to apply pressure. The Greek word carries the additional ideas of burden, affliction, and trouble, and is closely related to a word that means a rut or worn path. Do you get the idea? Tribulation is something that presses, rubs, and chafes relentlessly. Today we might liken it to stress, but it is really a much stronger concept than that. It would be like having your head in a spiritual vise grip with adversity continually tightening the screws.

Many of us don't know how to be overcomers, despite the fact that Jesus said He has overcome the world and promised us the victory (see Jn. 16:33). Second Corinthians 2:14 says, "But thanks be to God, who **always** leads us in triumphal procession in Christ and through us spreads every-where the fragrance of the knowledge of Him."

Where is the triumph in our lives? When people ask me that question, or when they recite a list of all their woes and problems, wringing their hands in despair and frustration, I like to say to them, "Well, you've simply got to 'Second Corinthians 10:5 it.' " This is not a flippant or pat answer, but a principle I have proven in my own life time and time again. Listen to Paul:

We demolish arguments and every pretension that sets itself up against the knowledge of God, and we take captive every thought to make it obedient to Christ (2 Corinthians 10:5).

When a negative or destructive thought comes, deal with it right then and there, before it digs a foothold. Just say to that thought, "I recognize you, you proud and lofty thing that would try to rise up in me against the true knowledge of Christ. Get out of here. Get off my case." It will.

The Hobble of Persecution

Persecution carries the thought of relentless pursuit. A persecutor simply will not let you alone. Persecution be-cause of the Word of God, harassment simply for being a Christian, are experiences we in the western world still know little about. From time to time we may experience it to a small degree at home or on the job; perhaps we'll get a cold shoulder or a mocking comment. Severe verbal or physical persecution is a reality that few of us have ever encountered. It is quite common in most of the rest of the world, however, and I believe the day is ahead when it will become real for us as well.

No matter when we face persecution, or what form it takes, God has made a powerful promise to us through which we can endure it:

"No weapon forged against you will prevail, and you will refute every tongue that accuses you. This is the heritage of the servants of the Lord, and this is their vindication from Me," declares the Lord (Isaiah 54:17).

Notice it does not say that there won't be any weapons forged against us, but that those that are made will not prevail. Through God's power we will be able to answer every accusation made against us. This is the heritage God has given us as His children. Our defense and preservation are in His hands.

Although persecution may come in human form and with human voices, in reality we will not be refuting flesh and blood. The real persecutor is our spiritual adversary and accuser, satan. Words of both life and death are released into the heavenly realm around us. Words of cursing and derision, put-downs, lies, words of persecution and defamation, and all other sorts of garbage that go out against us as individuals, go into the heavenly realm, and I believe that it is our right and authority as children of God to refute those words in the Name of the Lord Jesus Christ of

Nazareth. If we do that, by God's power they will have no effect on our lives.

Consider the wonderful promise Jesus made:

Blessed are you when people insult you, persecute you and falsely say all kinds of evil against you because of Me. Rejoice and be glad, because great is your reward in heaven, for in the same way they persecuted the prophets who were before you (Matthew 5:11-12).

When persecution heads our way, when lies, slander, and other evil things are said about us because we are Christians, we can rest and take comfort in the reality that there is a great reward in Heaven for us. But the whole point is, if we are not standing strong in who we are in Christ, then the persecution that comes will be a hobble that keeps us from running.

The Hobble of Worldly Cares

In the parable of the sower recorded in Mark 4:3-20, Jesus says that the thorny ground represents the "cares of this world" (KJV). The Greek word for "cares" means distractions, and it carries the idea of being double-minded. If we are caught up in the cares of the world, we are anxious and easily distracted, and we brood unnecessarily. This has nothing to do with being smart and accountable and concerned about the things that we are responsible for, but with being anxious beforehand about the affairs of daily life.

That kind of care is sin because we are told in the Word not to be anxious about anything, but to present everything to God in prayer, so that His peace will fill us (see Phil. 4:6-7). If we want God's peace, we have to give

Him our anxieties. This is something we have to do over and over again because of our own weakness. If we would nurture this, and learn to walk in an abiding, moment-by-moment "now" walk with Him, it would revolutionize our lives.

When the Word says to us, "do not be anxious," it doesn't mean for us not to be conscientious in our planning. Rather, it means not to let worry, care, and anxiety rule our lives. We are not to fix our eyes on it or become consumed with it. Instead, we are to fix our eyes on Jesus, and everything else will fall into place.

When we learn to "seek first the kingdom of God and His righteousness" (see Mt. 6:33), we will cut from our feet the hobble of worldly cares. Our Father's love provides for both our daily needs and our special needs.

The Hobble of Worldly Desires

There are many beautiful and wonderful things that we can enjoy: good theater, good music, beauty in nature, good literature, fine art. Those are not what I mean by worldly desires. The worldly desires that hobble us are our longings, our priorities—the things that continually take pre-eminence over intimacy with God and walking in the Spirit.

Sometimes when I ask people to list their priorities, many times, if they are honest, they discover that the things of the faith, of the Spirit, and of the Kingdom of God are nowhere near the top of their lists. We are so busy putting other things in priority, and we have so many obligations, that time for the things of God take second, third, fourth, or umpteenth place. No wonder God seems so far away; no wonder there is no spiritual power in our lives.

We need to cut the hobbles that hinder us; we must be alert for the snares that threaten us. The only way to do so is by abiding with Jesus moment by moment, and acknowledging Him as Lord, our constant Shield and Fortress, our Strength, our Hope, our Shepherd, our Lover, our Savior, our Healer, our Wisdom, our Life.

Chapter 11

Keeping Your Equilibrium

The creation waits in eager expectation for the sons of God to be revealed. ... We know that the whole creation has been groaning as in the pains of childbirth right up to the present time (Romans 8:19,22).

All creation groans and waits for the sons of God to be revealed. "Sons of God" is not a sexist phrase; it simply means mature children of God. Verse 14 of the same chapter says that the sons of God are those who are led by the Spirit of God. All creation is waiting in eager expectation for the unveiling of mature, Spirit-filled, Spirit-led children of God. In the same way, could it be expressed that thousands in the Church are groaning in anticipation of the revealing and releasing of the daughters of God into their God-appointed callings and giftings. I know from experience the great sigh that is inside the hearts of multitudes of women.

One of the strongest desires of my heart is to awaken, equip, and release women into their calling and full potential in the Body of Christ. There is a crying need for a greatly increased understanding of God's Word and His heart toward liberty for women in the Church.

Another desperate need for Christian women is to lift from them the weights of bondage, shame, and perceived inabilities they struggle under so that they may come alongside men and declare the Word of God in doing the works of the Kingdom. God anoints and appoints His daughters to prophesy, preach, teach, and assume God-given roles right alongside His sons, both within the local church and in the Body of Christ at large, at all times expressing humility in character and trusting God for His promotion.

A third need is for women in the Church to be encouraged to be reconcilers, peacemakers, and hope-givers, releasing words of life and nurture to tired leaders and congregations.

The Christian women who will succeed in these things will be the ones who are godly and well-balanced—women who can keep their equilibrium in an off-balance world. That is not easy. It requires commitment, hard work, and sacrifice; yet God has called us to nothing less. We need to take a close look, then, at the qualities of a godly, balanced woman, called and equipped to release life into the Body of Christ.

Hindrances to Godly Balance

The qualities that will make us godly and balanced will come not from the world around us, but from the depths of our spirits, souls, and emotions. They will be manifested from within. This is important, because our actions come from either wholeness within or carnality and disruption from without. Inner wholeness brings peace, balance, and stability. Carnality, or living according to the flesh, produces fear, insecurity, confusion, and weakness. The qualities displayed in our lives will be determined by which nature we feed: our spiritual nature in Christ, or our carnal nature in the world.

There are many things that can hinder the development of godly balance in women. One is the spirit of **competition**, where women feel pressured to measure up, to perform equal to or better than men in order to be accepted. This is a very unsettling place to be. It is hard to move out in a balanced manner when you feel that you are constantly under scrutiny with someone just waiting for you to mess up.

There is rampant in the Body of Christ today a dreadful manifestation of competition, self-protection, lack of trust, and jealousy among women. Although everything may appear to be "sugar and spice and everything nice" on the surface, behind the facades lie attitudes and emotions that are far from godly—attempts to manipulate and control people and circumstances.

Another major hindrance is that many women feel **imprisoned by the past**. Guilt, shame, regrets, abuse, or any number of other negative experiences can become shackles that hold women in the past, control the present, and offer little hope for the future. That is not God's desire for any of His children. He placed us in His Body to pour out to one another in freedom, grace, and joy.

A third hindrance to godly balance is a **carnal lifestyle**. Paul discusses in chapters 2 and 3 of First Corinthians three kinds of people: the natural man, the spiritual man, and the carnal man. The natural man is man in his fallen state, lost and enslaved to sin, without God or spiritual discernment. The spiritual man has been set free in Christ and lives a life of spiritual victory by walking consistently in the knowledge and Spirit of God. The carnal man is a Christian who, although set free in Christ, is walking and living primarily according to the sinful flesh (see 1 Cor. 2:11–3:3). It is impossible to live a godly, balanced life and walk according to the flesh.

Abigail: Portrait of a Balanced Woman

First Samuel chapter 25 tells the story of a remarkable woman named Abigail who displayed many characteristics of a balanced, godly woman. Her name means "source of joy," and I believe the meaning of her name was reflected in her life. The story is too long to quote here, so a brief synopsis will have to suffice. Let me encourage you to read the full account for an even better understanding.

Abigail was an intelligent and beautiful woman who was married to a very wealthy but ill-natured man named Nabal. They lived in the desert region of Paran near Mount Carmel. David and 600 men with him were living in the same region because King Saul was seeking to kill David. David and his men, all excellent fighters, protected the people of the area, including Nabal and his household, from harm. During sheep-shearing season, David sent ten of his men with a respectful request for Nabal to share some of his food and provisions with them. Nabal refused the request, treating David and his men with contempt. He was ill-mannered and ungrateful, and his behavior was quite contrary to acceptable standards and customs of hospitality. David responded in hot anger, and he and 400 of his men prepared to kill Nabal and all the male members of his family.

Some of Nabal's servants reported these things to Abigail, assuring her of the integrity and upright behavior of David and his men on their behalf. Abigail lost no time. She gathered a large supply of bread, wine, sheep, grain, raisins, and figs, loaded them on donkeys, and, without informing

Nabal, rode off to meet David and his band. When she approached David, Abigail humbled herself before him and interceded on behalf of herself, her husband, and their household. She asked David to pay no attention to the insult her husband had given, and to stay his hand from taking his own vengeance. She expressed confidence and faith that God would raise up for David a royal dynasty, and would protect him. David responded with favor to Abigail's appeal. His anger cooled, and he respected and honored the woman who had so boldly come to him and helped him refrain from wreaking vengeance in anger.

Abigail returned home with David's promise of peace, to find Nabal having a drunken banquet. The next morning, when he was sober, she told him what she had done. Nabal's heart "failed him and he became like a stone" (verse 37). Ten days later, the Lord struck Nabal and he died. Upon hearing the news of Nabal's death, David rejoiced that he had not taken vengeance and that the Lord had dealt with Nabal. Shortly thereafter, David invited Abigail to become his wife.

This story reveals a number of remarkable character traits in Abigail. First, she was **an intelligent woman of integrity**. Integrity means an unimpaired condition, an uncompromising adherence to a code of moral values. This was her reputation. She was a woman of her word, one who could be trusted. She was a woman of integrity.

Secondly, Abigail was **respected** by everyone who knew her. This was clearly the case with the servants and household staff, because it was to her they came with the problem. They knew better than to approach Nabal. They were confident that Abigail would know what to do. The servants expected authority and responsibility from her.

It is also obvious from his response that David felt great respect for her.

Abigail was **resourceful**. When you consider all the provisions she had to gather and the quick thinking required to collect everything that David and his men would need, it is clear that she was a good organizer. Her staff also must have responded well to her because they gathered an enormous amount of supplies very quickly.

Abigail was **single-minded**. The Bible says she made haste. She had a clear purpose and wasted no time. She was sharply focused and knew exactly what she needed to do. She was decisive and free of the practice of second-guessing. She moved out with deliberation.

Abigail was **full of wisdom**. She was wise in the ways and workings of God. She knew about Saul's attempts to kill David. She also knew that God's purpose was to make David king of Israel. She had insight that lay beyond merely human understanding. Abigail trusted that God's purpose would come to pass at His proper timing.

Abigail had **courage**. Courage is mental or moral strength to confront or withstand danger, fear, or difficulty. First of all, it took courage to confront David. His reputation was well known. He was a fighting man, and when he was on the warpath he went all out. Second, she displayed courage when she reported all of this to Nabal. Her heart was probably beating furiously when she approached her husband after he was sober. From the description of him in the Bible, it is easy to imagine that Nabal was verbally and emotionally abusive to Abigail, and very possibly physically abusive as well. He was not a very approachable man. Her confronting him took courage.

Abigail was **diplomatic**. She was able to employ tact and conciliation. Diplomacy is an ability that comes from the heart and goes along with wisdom. Bluntness may be an expression of the truth, but it doesn't win hearts. Even though she herself had done no wrong, she said to David, "My lord, let the blame be on me alone" (1 Sam. 25:24). She was willing to stand as a mediator, in the place of her husband. She did not have any hidden agenda or excuses or denials about the situation, but was willing to come forth publicly for the sake of others.

Abigail displayed **humility**. Humility means having a right opinion of yourself. Another word for humility is **meekness**. Meekness is humility that is considerate, unassuming, and gentle. In the New Testament, Jesus is referred to as meek (see Mt. 11:29 KJV). This quality has nothing to do with weakness. In Jesus' case, meekness meant the power of humble wisdom and penetrating love. The Greek word was used to refer to a horse that had been tamed— power under perfect control. This is the kind of meekness, the kind of humility, that Abigail had.

So here we have them, character traits of godly balance that would grace any woman: integrity, respect, resourcefulness, single-mindedness, wisdom, courage, diplomacy, and humility. Do such characteristics seem out of touch with today's reality, or hopelessly out of reach? Remember that the Bible promises us that nothing is impossible with God (see Lk. 1:37). Anything that we believe He can do and wants to do, and that we allow Him to do, He will do.

Spiritual Qualities of a Godly Woman

In addition to the character traits displayed by Abigail, there are other spiritual qualities of a balanced, godly woman.

A godly woman is **a Spirit-filled woman**. She continually allows the Spirit of God to fill her and form her life. Romans 12:1 tells us to offer our bodies as living sacrifices, holy and pleasing to God, as a spiritual act of worship. This is a day-by-day, moment-by-moment submission. In light of everything that Jesus did for us, the least we can do for Him is submit our bodies to Him. Notice it doesn't say to offer our spirits. Our spirits are already united as one with Him (see 1 Cor. 6:17). If we submit ourselves to Jesus and allow the Spirit to fill us consistently, He will manifest His life, His righteousness, His power, and His gifts through us.

A godly woman is **a Spirit-transformed woman**. Romans 12:2 tells us to no longer be conformed to the world's pattern, but be transformed by the renewing of our minds, and in that way discern God's pleasing and perfect will. One of the Holy Spirit's functions is to renew our minds, and He uses the Word of God to do it. We need our computers reprogrammed. The well-known computer slogan, "garbage in, garbage out," applies to our minds as well. What we feed into our minds is what will come out of them. If we feed on the things of the world, our minds will become worldly; if we feed on the things of God, our minds will become godly. We cannot know the things of God, understand the mind of God, or discern the will of God unless our minds are renewed and transformed into His likeness.

Galatians 5:16 says, "...live by the Spirit, and you will not gratify the desires of the sinful nature." We cannot walk in the Spirit and walk in the flesh at the same time. It won't work. Jesus said no one can serve two masters (see Mt. 6:24). So, walk in the Spirit. This means submitting ourselves to His power and control. If we were truly honest, we would see how tightly we control our own lives. If we found ourselves in that place of allowing Him to transform us by the renewing of our minds, we would truly begin walking in and after the things of the Spirit, and not be dominating, controlling, and self-serving. First Samuel 16:7 says, "...Man looks at the outward appearance, but the Lord looks at the heart." God spoke these words to the prophet Samuel as he began to minister according to his own "game plan." You and I need to get to the place where, as godly, balanced women, we so hear His voice that we move in His agenda, not our own.

We are always concerned about having an anointing to do the job He asks us to do. I learned a few years ago that anointing follows obedience follows hearing. God is responsible for the anointing. You and I are responsible for responding to and obeying what He asks us to do.

A godly woman is **fervent in the Spirit**. That means she is aglow and burning with the zeal of the Spirit of God. It is a fiery hot, living fervor. Are we women who are full of living fervor and who are fiery hot for the things of the Kingdom of God? That is quite the opposite of being dignified, cold, and unemotional. Be aglow and burning with the Spirit. I think a balanced godly woman will be one who is seething fiery hot for God. In a Christian context, this signifies a high spiritual temperature inflamed by the Holy Spirit. No one else can do this for you. It is between you, Jesus, and the Holy Spirit.

A godly woman is **full of godly wisdom**. She has the wisdom of God on display and expressed within and through her. First Corinthians 2:9-10 says, "...'No eye has seen, no ear has heard, no mind has conceived what God has prepared for those who love Him'—but God has revealed it to us by His Spirit." Human understanding cannot conceive, understand, or explain the things of God or what He is doing, but the children of God know, because He has revealed it to us by His Spirit. True wisdom is always of spiritual origin. As we mature as children of God, we will increase in His wisdom. Hebrews 5:11-14 talks about moving past the milk stage and being able to eat meat; it is about coming into adulthood or maturity because we have had our senses trained to discern what is from God and what is not. God gives us wisdom that matures our attitudes and actions as well as the gift of the word of wisdom, which is one of the tools of the Holy Spirit for ministry (see 1 Cor. 12:8 KJV).

A godly woman is **solidly grounded in the Word of God**. We need to be growing and maturing women who have a strong knowledge of God's Word, of who we are in Christ, and of who He is in us. We need to know what the Word says, what it means, and how to apply it in our lives so we can become all that Jesus has liberated us to be. Being grounded in the Word gives security. It gives understanding. It leads us to know God in an intimate and personal way. Through the Word we experience His love, and that enables us to share His love with others. We cannot share something we ourselves do not have.

A godly woman walks in the **assurance of her salvation**. We have been born again of the Spirit of God and the life of God. We are saved. We are new creatures in Christ. That fact must be settled in our hearts before we can ever mature in Him. John 5:24 says, "I tell you the truth, whoever hears My word and believes Him who sent Me has eternal life and will not be condemned; he has crossed over from death to life." Those are present tense verbs. For we who believe in Jesus as Savior and Lord, eternal life is a present reality, not just a future hope. First John 5:13 says we can know we have eternal life. The Lord wants us to be sure of this. He has given us His Spirit to testify with our spirits that we are children of God (see Rom. 8:16).

A godly woman is a **woman of vision**. It says in Proverbs that without vision, people perish (see Prov. 29:18 KJV). Godly women of vision have a strong sense of purpose and calling. They remain clearly focused with their eyes on Jesus. They also have the capacity to see beyond what is to what can be, in the mind and purpose of God. God has made us vessels to house His life, and wants us to pour out that life—and pour it out, and pour it out.

A godly woman is **pure in all her relationships**. If she is married, she enjoys that relationship with her husband and has come to understand and appreciate the wonderful intimacy that comes through true biblical submission. In a godly marriage, a husband and wife submit mutually to one another in love and self-sacrifice, in the same manner in which Christ gave Himself for His Church. A fully released woman enjoys a fruitful ministry because her husband does not feel threatened by it and encourages her. If she is single, God can enable her to enjoy that state tremendously. Whether single by choice, by lack of opportunity, or through divorce or widowhood, godly unmarried Christian women should be able to relate in a tremendous, wholesome way with both men and women.

A godly woman is **totally free of any feminist traits**. I believe that we need to be as feminine as we possibly can. Being feminine and being a feminist are not the same. A feminist agenda against men and a "jezebel" spirit of control, manipulation, and domination are ungodly and completely out of place in the Church. God has not called us to be militant feminists, but to be His daughters walking in the full inheritance, anointing, and calling that He has for us. In Christ there is neither male nor female (see Gal. 3:28). The women in the New Testament Church were released neither to dominate nor be dominated, but to work alongside the men in full respect and equality.

A godly woman is a **spiritually gifted woman**. She reveals in her life an ever-increasing fruitfulness as she works out her salvation in a daily intimate walk with Jesus and the ministry of the gifts of the Spirit. She is aware of her own giftings and seeks to minister accordingly in the place of service God opens up for her.

All of us as Christian, Spirit-filled women have been gifted by the Spirit of God for ministry and the building of the Body of Christ. He has created us with specific motivations and placed His spiritual, supernatural abilities within us so that the entire Church can be built up and established in Christ.

Motivational Gifts Are "What Make You Tick?"

God has placed inherent qualities within you that determine your strength, your commitment, and your enthusiasm toward life. They very much determine your approach to situations and other people, coloring all that you do.

Maybe you are a **perceiver** or are prophetically motivated. That does not necessarily mean that God has called you to be a prophet. You are like the eyes, ears, and nose of the Body. You can really smell things out. If you are walking closely with God, you are able to perceive His will in situations. Some people will think that you can look right through them, but you cannot. God reveals nothing to anyone except for the purpose of bringing a person into a closer walk with Him. You are generally a "black and white" person; there is no gray. You hate sin with a passion. You hate it in the world and you hate it in the Church. Most of all, you hate it within your own life. You are one God is calling to intercede much. Intercession is your escape valve from being too outspoken or blunt because you will share these passions and burdens with Him. You will spend much time in prayer and listening to God. With truth and compassion you will touch the hearts of others and bring conviction and restoration within the Body.

Maybe you are a **server**, the hands of the Body. The servant heart is your God-given motivation. If you are the hands of the Body, you are the one who gives practical assistance in all sorts of areas to keep the work of the ministry going. You are vital to the Body and should never deny your "Martha-type" heart as you delight in your Lord and simply love to help others.

Some of you are **teachers**. You are like the mind of the Body. You love to research the Scriptures, and when you speak and teach you are like a walking library or thesaurus bringing to life the truth of God's Word to people's understanding. That is a teacher motivation and will be there even if you've never been trained as a teacher.

If you are an **exhorter**, you are the mouth of the Body. You are also the feet because the Bible talks about the blessedness of the feet of those who bring good news (see Rom. 10:15). As an exhorter, you are an encourager, one who inspires personal growth, stimulates the faith of others, and motivates them to grow up spiritually so that when they face hardship they can be overcomers. A very positive person, you continually build others up and are a real peacemaker in the Kingdom.

Givers are the arms and supports for the other parts of the Body and other ministries. You are the ones who supply a lot of financial and material assistance to keep the ball rolling. God has placed you in the Body for moral support and encouragement of the Body through a generous heart. Very wise and frugal, you give far more than money though, pouring out love, time, energy, and possessions to others. A call to intercession is a strong quality within you.

Some of you may be **administrators**. As such, you are the shoulders and backbone of the work with a tremendous responsibility for keeping everybody organized and on target and for expanding other people's abilities, helping them plug in where they fit. Some of you are anointed initiators. There is nothing wrong with women being initiators. You are self-starters, able to delegate and encourage others. That does not mean being bossy. There is something inside you that just calls others to come alongside. You recognize the giftings in others and are able to prefer them, freely releasing them into their anointing. You do not feel threatened, protective, or jealous in any way when others begin moving out in their callings and their giftings. Rather than being fearful of being diminished yourself, you rejoice that they have found their places of abundance and fulfillment in the Kingdom.

If you are **mercy-motivated**, you are a compassionate person, the heart of the Body, able to extend personal and emotional comfort and identify with those who are in distress. With a huge capacity to give love, often ruled by your heart rather than your head, you intercede for others' needs regularly.

Each of us as believers has at least one of these motivational gifts. You may have high degrees of effectiveness in more than one, but one in particular will usually stand out. As you grow in your intimacy with God, learning to walk in the freedom and security of your place in Christ, you will grow in the awareness of your gifting and equipping for the ministry.

My heart as far as women in ministry is concerned is very simple: **Find a need and fill it**! There are too many hurting, wounded, hungry, lost people out there—people who need to see and hear the life of Christ manifested in and through us. They need to hear releasing words of life coming from women like you and me. Remember, doing the works of the Kingdom does not depend upon "committee approval." Your anointing and gifting will make room for you.

Dr. Fuchsia Pickett made a profound statement: "Where He guides, He provides; where He provides, He promotes; what He promotes, He protects. If He doesn't guide, then forget the rest of it...you don't have to promote yourself!"

Walk before the Lord and wait upon Him. Serve where He plants you. Joy and peace are the by-products of being in the place God would have you be and of doing what He has called you to do. The Lord will lead you to the place where you can pour out the divine river within you, releasing life—the resurrection life, the sin-defeating, satan-destroying eternal life—into the Body of Christ and into a dark, lost, and dying world.

Exciting titles

by Debby Jones and Jackie Kendall

LADY IN WAITING
by Debby Jones and Jackie Kendall.
This is not just another book for singles! With humor, honesty, and biblical truths, the authors help point women to *being* the right woman and not just finding the right man! With *Lady in Waiting*, any woman—married or single—will learn that only a relationship with Jesus will satisfy!
ISBN 1-56043-848-7 $9.99p

LADY IN WAITING Devotional Journal & Study Guide
by Debby Jones and Jackie Kendall.
You can keep the principles taught in *Lady in Waiting* in your heart by learning to apply them with this devotional journal and study guide. These questions, quotes, thoughts, and teachings will help you to become the woman of God that He designed you to be. You also can record your spiritual growth in a specially designed journal section. Don't miss this opportunity to become God's "Lady in Waiting"!
ISBN 1-56043-298-5 $7.99p

LUNATIC ON A LIMB WITH JESUS
by Jackie Kendall.
Do you ever feel like life has you dangling from a tree limb? Don't worry! You can survive—just look up to Jesus! Take one day at a time with this humorous, autobiographical devotional by the irrepressible Jackie Kendall. Discover how you can survive life's surprises and come out smiling!
ISBN 1-56043-306-X $9.99p

HOW TO AVOID A BOZO—*NEW VIDEO!*
Help for Finding God's Best in a Mate
by Jackie Kendall.
Do you want to find God's best—Mr. Right? Learn the differences between a man worth waiting for and a Bozo. Don't let your lover be a loser!
1 video ISBN 0-7684-0070-8 Retail $14.99

Available at your local Christian bookstore.

Internet: http://www.reapernet.com

D *Destiny Image*
New Releases

FLASHPOINTS OF REVIVAL
by Geoff Waugh.
Throughout history, revival has come to various countries and peoples.
Why those times? Why those people? Why not others? This book takes you
inside the hearts and minds of people who lived through the major revivals
of the past years. Discover how today's revivals fit into God's timeline of
awakenings.
ISBN 0-7684-1002-9 $9.99p

IN SEARCH OF REVIVAL
by Stuart Bell.
Will revival always look the same? Who will recognize it when it comes?
What part do we play in bringing revival to our areas? How do we sustain
revival? *In Search of Revival* details how you can position yourself for the
moving of God's Spirit. You'll see characteristics marking churches on their
own quest. Get ready to see revival in a whole new way!
ISBN 0-7684-1001-0 $9.99p

FOR GOD'S SAKE GROW UP!
by David Ravenhill.
It's time to grow up...so that we can fulfill God's purposes for us and for our
generation! For too long we've been spiritual children clinging to our mother's leg, refusing to go to school on the first day. It's time to put away child-
ish things and mature in the things of God—there is a world that needs to be
won to Christ!
ISBN 1-56043-299-3 $9.99p

USER FRIENDLY PROPHECY
by Larry J. Randolph.
Hey! Now you can learn the basics of prophecy and how to prophesy in a
book that's written for you! Whether you're a novice or a seasoned believer,
this book will stir up the prophetic gift God placed inside you and encourage you to step out in it.
ISBN 1-56043-695-6 $9.99p

Available at your local Christian bookstore.
Internet: http://www.reapernet.com
Prices subject to change without notice.   2:96

Destiny Image
Revival Books

IMAGES OF REVIVAL
by Richard and Kathryn Riss.
"Revival" means many things to many people. But what is real revival actually like? In this brief overview, the authors examine the many images of revivals that have occurred throughout the years. God's moves upon His people are exciting and sometimes unexpected. Learn how revival could come to your community!
ISBN 1-56043-687-5 $9.99p

SHARE THE FIRE
by Guy Chevreau.
Do you panic when you hear the word *evangelism*? Do you feel awkward "forcing" your opinions on another? All that changes when God abundantly and freely fills you with His Spirit! In *Share the Fire* you'll learn how God has intended evangelism to be: a bold and free work of Christ in you and through you!
ISBN 1-56043-688-3 $9.99p

THE CHURCH OF THE 3RD MILLENNIUM
by Marc Dupont.
Uncontrollable laughter, violent shaking, falling "under the Spirit"—can these things really be from God? Using examples from the ministries of Elijah, John the Baptist, and Jesus Himself, Marc Dupont shows that God often moves in ways that challenge traditional religious views or habits; He "offends the mind in order to reveal the heart." God's end-time Church shouldn't be satisfied with the status quo. We need to reach for more of God's Spirit—and not be surprised when He gives it to us!
ISBN 1-56043-194-6 $9.99p

GO INSIDE THE TORONTO BLESSING—*NEW VIDEO*
by Warren Marcus.
Award-winning filmmaker Warren Marcus takes you behind the scenes where you can experience a true look at this revival with footage that has never been filmed before. You will feel like you have a front row seat at the worship services. You will witness the special prayer time when many of the miracles occur. You will see unusual "manifestations"—like those reported in prior revivals. And you will hear first-person account after account of how God has dramatically changed people's lives in this revival.
1 video (approx. 60 min.) ISBN 0-7684-0082-1 Retail $19.99

Available at your local Christian bookstore.
Internet: http://www.reapernet.com
Prices subject to change without notice.   2:52